Zingerman's ®

guide to giving great service

Zingerman's®

guide to giving great service

by ari weinzweig

Zingerman's, Ann Arbor, Michigan, 2003

© Ari Weinzweig 2003

Second hardcover edition

2020 2019 2018 2017 5 4 3 2

Cover illustration: Ian Nagy
Design: Nicole Robichaud
Interior illustrations: Ian Nagy, Phil Stead, and Adam Forman

ISBN: 978-0-9893494-4-4

www.zingermanspress.com

Printed, bound, and warehoused locally, in southeastern Michigan.

Table of Contents

preface

"Don't open
a shop unless
you know how
to smile."
—Jewish proverb

We've been teaching service for so long now at
Zingerman's that it's hard for me to remember a day when
we didn't. When we got into business in 1982, Paul Saginaw
and I had only two other people on staff. And although all
four of us were working hard to give great service, I can
guarantee that we weren't doing formal training classes on
the subject. When you're a little start-up business, who has
the time? I know that we were too busy just waiting on
customers and doing what we needed to do to succeed, in
an industry where roughly 90% of new businesses go under
within their first year. At that point, we just did things that
seemed incredibly obvious to us: Be really nice to customers, smile, and get them what they want—enthusiastically,
energetically, and accurately; thank people for their business; work a million hours a week in the process; figure
that our employees would just pick it up from the way we
were doing it, and, well, the rest would take care of itself—

which is true and not true. It did work out and happily we're still going—and growing—strong. But it was far from that simple.

I guess I should back up a bit and share some background on Zingerman's: what it is, where we came from, and where we're going. While our reputation has spread across the country, the building in which the Deli got its origins is very small—a mere 1,300 square feet into which we managed to squeeze something like 24 seats at which our guests could sit and eat if they didn't want to take their food home with them. From day one we've focused our efforts on selling full-flavored traditionally made foods, including all sorts of sandwiches, traditional Jewish fare, cheeses, breads, olives, olive oils, and more. While we've added on to the Deli two times over the years, it's still a pretty darned small space. But thanks, I think, to our never-ending drive to improve the flavor of our food and the level of service we provide, our work to educate both staff and customers about what makes our food special, our commitment to our community, and the fact that we get to work with such great customers and superior staff members, we've steadily grown that little Deli into a unique, fun-to-work-in organization that's been recognized all over the country for many years now.

What started out in '82 with a couple of staff members and twenty spots to sit and eat is now a $25 million a year organization that includes eight different Zingerman's businesses and about 400 staff members (see update on page 120). Today the Zingerman's Community of Businesses include the Deli, Bakehouse, Catering, and Mail Order; Zingerman's Creamery makes fresh handmade cream cheese (the way it was done 100 years ago); Zingerman's Coffee Company roasts the best beans we can find; Zingerman's Roadhouse is a full-service sit-down restaurant serving traditional regional American food, beers, and wines; and ZingTrain provides training and consulting services to share the Zingerman's Experience with other business folks around the country. Each of the businesses has received recognition and acclaim on its own—over the years we've been named Retailer of the Year three times by specialty food publications and one of 25 of the World's Best Food Markets. We've been featured in an array of food and business magazines and have presented what we do at all sorts of conferences and educational forms. In 2003, Training and Development magazine named ZingTrain one of Training's New Guard. The Creamery's cream cheese took a blue ribbon in its very first year at the American Cheese Society judging. Our Mail Order catalog has won a number of national awards. And the organization overall has garnered acclaim as well, being named the Coolest Small Company in America by *Inc.* magazine in 2003 and given the National Leadership Award by *Gourmet News* magazine in 2004.

It's pretty clear that our approach to service as been a huge part of making all of this possible. Our success and steady growth over the years is a testament to the fact that what we're teaching and operating on is the fact that service really does work. And it works in almost every venue you can imagine—today, we provide services that include everything from single cups of coffee to huge catering jobs, from consulting projects to corned beef sandwiches. We do mail order by phone and over the internet, and we work as a wholesaler selling breads, baked goods, coffee, and handmade cheeses to shops and restaurants all over the country. The great thing about our service training is that it works equally well in every single one of those settings.

Before I go any further, lest you think that I'm some sort of natural-born service provider, I should make it clear that I did not grow up with this stuff. To be honest, I can't even remember anyone in my family talking about it. Education. Religion. Politics. Sports. Those topics I remember. Service? Not really. The closest thing I can recall were regular mentions of how hard life was working in a service industry. My grandparents once owned a laundry on the Southside of Chicago, and I don't ever recall them reminiscing over it with anything resembling affection. All I remember is hearing, with great regularity, that the laundry was hot in the summer. Unbearably hot. Having listened to their laments for so many of my formative years left me with the belief that the service world was not a desirable place to be. So when I started to work in restaurants after getting my history degree from the University of Michigan, I had some serious internal work to do to truly make peace with the idea that what I was doing was a worthwhile way of life.

why the zingerman's approach?

Unlike our earliest days at the Deli, we now actively and formally teach service all the time. We do regular classes for our staff. We travel around the country—and even to Europe—to teach it to others (every kind of business from health care to health foods, from booksellers to roller coaster companies). Through our training and consulting business, ZingTrain, we teach it in a two-day seminar, right here in Ann Arbor, attended by service providers from all over the country and from every walk of life. While each venue gets its own customized agenda, we teach the same approach in every single setting. Speaking of approach, there are probably about 800 other books you could buy on this subject. I've read dozens of them myself over the last 10 or 15 years, many of which I'll happily recommend. So that said, why would the world want one more? Because the way we teach service here at Zingerman's seems to be so different from the way most others do it. And—much more importantly—because the method we teach really works. Everyone here at Zingerman's and around the country who's put our systems in place has been able to get great results, solid staff buy-in, and very positive long-term customer relationships.

In terms of translating what we've believed from the beginning into a model that genuinely works in the real world, there are five major parts to what we do. While many organizations do one part or the other, my belief is that all great service providers do all five well.

1. We teach it.

Without effective training, great service is just one more good idea that never really happens. We're relentless about our service training. The good news is that there's no reason others can't be just as dedicated. I'll guarantee that it's worth the effort—this stuff really works! When someone finishes our training, they actually know what we expect with regard to service. And—through our classes, seminars and training materials—we've given them a series of very tangible tools with which to make it happen. The more we teach it, the more effectively we can—and do—live it.

2. We define it.

Of course, in order to really teach service effectively, you have to actually define what it is that you're looking for. Treating service as a generic, if desirable, concept isn't going to help anyone improve the quality of their work. What helps is that we've given a clear definition of service—what we refer to as a "recipe"—that works. Our approach isn't just a theory developed in a fancy think tank somewhere; it's what we've been doing every day of every week for over two decades. I know it works because we use it with great success every day, and because I've seen others we've taught successfully adapt what we do to their own organizations, with a modicum of effort.

3. We live it.

At the end of the day, this is what really counts. Every organization talks about the importance of service these days.
We're hardly the only place in the country that teaches the
subject, nor are we unique in giving it definition. I think
that what sets us apart (and the many others who give
great service out there) is that after defining it and teaching it, we actually devote enormous energy to walking our
talk. Mind you, we never get it perfect. But we constantly
work at it, perfecting the alignment between the way we
teach it, the way we define it, and the way we live it.

4. We measure it.

Service measurement provides
the service world with the
same sort of helpful data
that financial statements
provide you with for
your money. Quite sim-
ply, measurement gives
us a scorecard for ser-
vice, a commonly shared language about how we're doing,
where we're succeeding and
where we're falling short. It helps
us differentiate between our personal experiences of
service and what the data says actually happened over the
course of an entire week or month.

5. We reward it

It's imperative that we effectively recognize and reward those in our organizations who go out and give great service. Both formal and informal reward systems will go a long way toward helping to build the service-oriented culture and the effective service delivery we're so committed to.

These five elements of our service success—teaching, defining, living, measuring, and rewarding—form the heart of this book. What we've done—through lots of trial and error, learning from others, and effective recovery when we screw up—is to create a learnable, usable and very teachable angle on service that will work in any industry, in an organization of any size, in wholesale and retail, in for-profit and not-for-profit, in ma and pa shops, and in publicly-traded multinationals.

teaching it

effective training on the art of giving great service

"Good service pleases both the giver and the recipient by the beauty of the performance, thereby enhancing life and adding value to an event that would otherwise be only a transaction."
—James Hillman, *Kinds of Power*

For a few minutes, imagine that you're here for one of our service classes. You've got a good cup of coffee on hand (or, if you're like me, a large pot of tea), and a great, traditional bagel from the Bakehouse spread with some of the Creamery's handmade (no vegetable gum) cream cheese. Imagine there are about 15 other folks on hand, too. Look around and you'll see some front-line staffers, a few managers, a bookkeeper, even a partner perhaps; everyone here goes through the same service training regardless of previous experience, seniority, or job title.

(If you're impatient and you just want to go straight to the service recipes, you can flip to page 37. But if you want to get the full in-depth approach to our service training just keep reading.)

the zingerman's business perspective chart

In all too many organizations, service is addressed as if it were only minimally related to the rest of the work everyone does. In our experience, training is infinitely more effective when we can show our staff how service fits into the context of our overall organizational activity. So with that in mind, we begin every class by going over what we call "The Zingerman's Business Perspective Chart."

This is a tool we developed back in the mid-'90s in an effort to get—and help keep—our priorities straight. As you'll see in a second, service plays a part in every element of it. For years now we've used it in every single bit of classroom training we do. I swear by the thing. I bring it up here because I think that to make it an effective part of an organization, great service has to be well-woven into the fabric of every aspect of the Business Perspective Chart: mission, vision, bottom lines, systems, culture, and guiding principles.

Zingerman's
business perspective

the zingerman's experience

Vision
↓
principles
culture ← → systems
↓
results
great food! great service!
great finance!

the zingerman's experience

zingerman's mission statement

In the spring of 1993, we put together a work group of managers, staff, and owners and set out to put to paper a statement of what Zingerman's is all about. Six months and many, many hours later—after getting about 70 or 80 different staff members involved—we came up with the Mission Statement and Guiding Principles that we still use today. Our Mission Statement reads like this:

> we share the zingerman's experience
> selling food that makes you happy
> giving service that makes you smile
> in passionate pursuit of our mission
> showing love and care in all our actions
> to enrich as many lives as we possibly can.

In my experience, most mission statements quickly become little more than meaningless poetry, often hanging out front for customers to read (we don't post ours in public), and of little value to those in the organization. But in truth, the mission statement is a very valuable tool, teacher, and guide. It answers some basic but incredibly important questions that are easy to ignore in the day-to-day, but also ones that, when answered, make all of our work more meaningful and more effective: "What do we do?" "Who are we?" "Why are we here?" "For whom are we doing it?"

"Service that fully satisfies is done with
no expectation of return, and is freely chosen."
—Peter Block, *Stewardship*

What do we do? This was the most challenging part
of writing the Mission Statement. After many hours of
hand-wringing and paper-shredding, we arrived at
the conclusion that what we want to do is deliver an
exceptional and unique experience. Sure, we do lots
of things: We make great products, we give exceptional
service, we do a lot of training, tasting, packaging, and
cleaning. We do our share of administrative activity,
too. But all of that stuff—the food, the service, the atmo-
sphere, the staff, the signs, the information, the fun, the
craziness—it's really only successful when it's delivered
in the context of bringing a great overall experience to
our customers, our staff, and our community.

Note that, in this context, our Mission Statement starts
to address the issue of service right from the start of
our work:

"We share the Zingerman's Experience, selling food that
makes you happy, giving service that makes you smile..."

Who are we? We are the people who work here in the
Zingerman's Community of Businesses. New and old,
baker and bread seller, dishwasher and dreamer, accoun-
tant and assistant manager, owner and off-site caterer,
sandwich maker and sign maker. Regardless of rank,
seniority, age, or anything else, we are all responsible
for making the Zingerman's Experience—including our
service—a reality for every single individual with whom
we interact.

Why do we do it? "To enrich as many lives as we possibly can." We believe that if we do our jobs well, we can leave our community, our staff and everyone else we work with a little better off than when we got here.

For whom are we doing it? For our guests, for ourselves, for our community, and for the folks who make the great foods we work with.

In my view, the Mission Statement works like the North Star. No matter how lost or frustrated we may feel on any given day, it's always there, much like the North Star, to help give us a general sense of direction. We can always find it, even in the dark and even when we're feeling confused. On the other hand, we'll never actually "arrive at" a complete fulfillment of the Mission Statement. Like the North Star, no matter how long and how hard we walk toward it, it will still be way out front helping to guide us. It's a lifelong organizational path, not something that's measurable or time-constrained. It offers us a broad sense of direction, but it doesn't tell us very clearly what it's going to look like when we get to where we're going. That's where vision comes in.

Vision

As we use the term here, "vision" is a picture of what things are going to look like when we successfully arrive at where we're going and things are working really, really well. In other words, if you were sitting on a magic carpet floating up above your organization, maybe five years down the road, and you could see success, what would it look like? What would be happening? How big would the organization be?

What would it be known for? What does the
community say about it? What does the
press say about you? How would people be
dealing with each other inside the
organization? Specifically, what
would the service look like?
How would it be special?

In the context of service, the vision
question would be: "What does it look like when great
service is happening in my organization?" If you want to
take things further, don't stop there. Keep your visioning
work going in order to detail how your staff feels about
service, how the community talks about it, how the
industry recognizes you for it, how the leaders live it,
and so on.

The actual point in time that you choose is up to you;
it could be a year down the road or it could be ten years.
It could be ten minutes. There's no "right" time frame to
use for effective visioning. The point is, quite simply, that
if you want to be successful in any venture—large or
small, business or personal—you've got to know what
it's going to look like when you get where you're going,
otherwise you're sure to spend a lot of time wandering
around. Worse still, you're going to waste a lot of organizational energy while everyone around you either comes
up with their own vision or waits around for you to come
up with yours. A vision—whether it's for service, the organization overall or anything else—must be both inspiring
and strategically sound. One without the other won't cut
it. A successful vision also needs to be documented.
When it's not put on paper, it's too nebulous, too easy to

alter in conversation, too easy to back away from when things get tough. Putting it in writing adds power, makes it more real, and makes it significantly more likely that you're going to succeed. Lastly, the vision—whether of great service or anything else—has to be communicated. If you've got a really inspiring vision but no else knows what it is, you're not likely to get very far with it.

results On 3 bottom Lines: great food, great service, and great finance

In my fantasy, I'd sit down with a nice pot of tea, kick back, relax, maybe read a good book or two, take a long restful nap, and then wake up in a few years to find that our vision of greatness had been fulfilled. (Sounds good, doesn't it?) But I've learned the hard way that life just doesn't work like that. If we are actually going to make our vision a reality, we've got to track measurable, meaningful, bottom-line results on a daily, weekly, monthly, and annual basis in order to make sure that we're staying pretty much on course.

At Zingerman's, we measure our success by not one, but three, bottom lines:

1) Bring great food to our customers.
2) Give great service to everyone we interact with, both externally and internally.
3) Deliver great financial performance to the organization.

For us to feel successful, we must make our targets in all three areas. Just as we've got to deliver excellent profit and loss statements and a strong balance sheet to demonstrate financial success, we've got to come through with strong, well-quantified food and service scores at the same time.

In my experience, this view is very different from the way other organizations address this issue; most see service merely as a vehicle toward attainment of a financial end, not a bottom-line result in and of itself. Mind you, there's nothing wrong with using service as a strategic tool; in fact, I think it's quite sound. Better service is likely to improve your standing in the marketplace, keep customers coming back, spread positive word-of-mouth messages through your community, and so on. But my belief is that if you told most organizations that conclusive new studies showed that consumers no longer cared much about it, service would be dropped like every other trendy technique ever tried. For us, that's not an option.

Having great service as a bottom line sends a meaningful message to everyone in our organization that we are committed to walking our talk. For openers, our emphasis on the three bottom lines gives us a quick tool to evaluate our time and energy investment: If any one of us is spending significant energy on something that isn't contributing to one or more of our bottom lines, then it's probably not a great investment of our time. On the other hand, because service is one of our bottom lines, investing in work that will reap solid returns in that area—but only small financial or food gains—is still likely a good move for us.

Of course, lots of things go on while we're working to hit those bottom lines. That's what you see in the middle of the Business Perspective Chart.

Guiding Principles

Guiding principles define the way we relate to each other, our community, our suppliers, and our customers, all the while helping us to hit our bottom lines en route to making our vision a reality. Other terms you might use would be "ethics" or "values." At Zingerman's, our principles talk about our commitments to creating a great place to work, to giving back to our community, to rewarding long-term relationships, to each other's success, and to having fun while we're working. Specific to the subject at hand, our Guiding Principles address our commitment to providing great service to each other as well as to our guests. They talk about providing service to our community.

Throughout, they address the importance of service in our day-to-day work. Here's a quick look at the "service" section of our Guiding Principles:

"If great food is the lock, great service is the key. Great service at Zingerman's means:

"We go the extra mile for our guests, giving exceptional service to each of them. We are committed to giving great service—meeting the guests' expectations and then

See page 101 for the entire detailed list of our Guiding Principles.

exceeding them. Great service like this is at the core of the Zingerman's Experience. Our guests always leave with a sense of wonderment at how we have gone out of our way to make their experience at Zingerman's a rewarding one.

"**Our bottom line is derived from customer satisfaction.** Customer satisfaction is the fuel that stokes the Zingerman's fire. If our guests aren't happy, we're not happy. To this end, we consistently go the extra mile—literally and figuratively—for our guests. The customer is never an interruption in our day. We welcome feedback of all sorts. We constantly reevaluate our performance to better accommodate our customers. Our guests leave happy or satisfied. Each of us takes full responsibility for making our guest's experience an enjoyable one, before, during, and after the sale.

"At Zingerman's, we believe that giving great service is an honorable profession. Quality service is a dignified and honorable pursuit. We take great pride in our ability to provide our guests and our staff with exceptional service. Service is about giving and caring for those around us."

Systems

As we define the term, "systems" are the way that we say we do things, the way we say "it is" in our organization—

it could be payroll processing forms, recipes in the kitchen, procedures for packing orders at our Mail Order business, and more. Like every organization with more than 20 or so people, we have lots of systems at Zingerman's.

From a service standpoint, systems need to be designed to meet and then exceed customers' expectations. They need to create a structure in which accuracy and attention to detail are stressed over and over again. Reviewing each element of one's systems, and identifying all of the ways in which customer service can suffer or be improved, can be a big step toward upgrading service quality. Having great attitudes while working with poorly designed or poorly followed systems is better than having bad attitudes with bad systems, but the optimal situation occurs when both attitude and systems are geared toward giving great service.

culture

If the systems are the way we say things are supposed to work, then the culture is the every day reality of life. In essence, the culture is the personality of the organization. And just as each of us has individual strengths and weaknesses in our personalities, sos too do our organizations. Hey, we live in the real world, so we know that despite our best efforts, systems are never implemented 100% of the time. It's a normal part of organizational life that systems, culture, and principles can quickly come into conflict if we're not careful.

The obvious social example of this is the speed limit on the highway. Everyone knows that speed limit signs say

"The best way to find yourself is to lose yourself in the service of others." Mahatma Gandhi

"70 miles per hour." But everyone also knows that the "real" speed limit is that you drive as fast as you want unless there's a cop. Cruise down the road at 85 mph (in Michigan, at least) until you see that dome light on the side of the road, and then you very quickly slooooooow down! Take note, of course, that these aren't outlaws and brigands I'm talking about. They're well-respected and upstanding citizens. This obvious violation of the law is so unremarkable only because our culture sees speeding as perfectly acceptable—if, at times, finable—behavior. Take note that it's infinitely easier to rewrite a system than it is to really change the culture of an organization. Rules can be modified with a quick memo, but changing the culture takes a coherent vision, effective communication, years of stubborn persistence, relentless follow up, and probably a little luck. Witness the difficulty in eliminating racial discrimination from our society, decades after Congress and the courts took action to guarantee civil rights. When there are gaps like this between our systems and our culture (or between our systems and principles, or principles and culture), we believe—and actively teach—that it's the responsibility of everyone in our organization to work to get them back into alignment.

service self-assessment

One very practical exercise you can do is to rate your organization on the role that service plays in each of the six elements in the Business Perspective Chart.

On a scale of 1 to 5 (5 being the highest possible score you can give) rate your organization or department on how well it has great service integrated into your:

Mission

Vision

Bottom Line Results

Systems

Culture

Principles

Ultimately the culture—not the staff handbook, the CEO's position papers, or the company's marketing materials—is the best indicator of the quality of service in any organization. What do the folks who work with you say about service when you're not around? Do they tell their friends and family what great service means to them? Do they discuss service quality over lunch? (By the way, this is one subject that I like to hear complaining about: When I hear our staff moaning about the quality of the service they got elsewhere, it tells me that they've successfully internalized our service standards.)

why we give great service

When we actually kick into the content of our training, we always start by asking the group to answer the seemingly innocuous question: "Why even bother giving great service, anyway?"

The answer probably seems so self-evident that most places doing service training don't even bother to ask it. But sometimes the obvious questions are the most important ones; we take time to go through them because we believe it's essential that our staff understand the value in giving great service. And while it may seem clear to you and me, it's rarely apparent until you answer the question with the trainees. As we go through it, you can see their level of connection grow. They get more alert and become part of the process instead of just being lectured to (or, worse still, having to watch a service speech on video...it makes me tired just thinking about it). When a staff member understands the "why" of great service, he or she is a lot more invested in making it happen than they are when "service with a smile" is merely one more mandate from the "main office." All told, we'll usually list about seven or eight solid reasons to give great service.

1. Great service makes us something special.

Face the facts: We need customers far more than they need us. In an era of ever-increasing sameness, something as simple as a smile, the competent delivery of goods, or even just a little enthusiasm can make a lasting positive impression on customers. Though Zingerman's may be a valued component of our community, we hardly have a monopoly on bread, brownies, sandwiches, or scones. In fact, when it comes right down to it, we really don't have anything that can't be found in a somewhat-comparable form, in dozens of different shops within ten miles of us. To compound our challenge, there's really nothing we sell that anyone actually needs.

If we were to close up tomorrow, life in Ann Arbor might be a bit less interesting, but it would proceed just fine. Some people might be sad, others might even mourn, but they aren't going to roll up the sidewalks and exile everyone back to the suburbs. In an economy where there's more and more competition for customers' dollars, great service really does differentiate us from our competitors.

2. Great service is sound marketing.

You don't have to get an MBA to know that the best advertising is done by word-of-mouth. In a world where customer interactions are often downright dismal, actually getting superior service has become a memorable event for most people, one that they like to talk about often. I'm happy to say that at Zingerman's we have customers who still share stories of the times that we went the extra mile for them 10 or 15 years ago. Many tell these tales the same way grandparents smile and share fond stories of their grandchildren. This sort of positive personal message is worth more than thousands and thousands of dollars in marketing.

3. Good service keeps customers coming back.

Both formal statistical studies and all my years of hands-on, face-to-face experience lead me to the same conclusion: Customers who receive high-quality product but poor service are unlikely to give a shop a second shot. They simply spend their money somewhere else the next time. By contrast, surprisingly high numbers of clients who've gotten great service but received substandard product will return to give the business another opportunity to take care of them.

According to Janelle Barlow and Dianna Maul's *Emotional Value: Creating Strong Bonds with Your Customers:*

• Only 14% of customers who switch providers do it because they were unhappy with the quality of the product—most all make the move because they were dissatisfied with the service they'd received.

• Nearly three-quarters of all customer purchases are made by repeat purchasers.

• The cost of gaining a new customer is nearly five times that of keeping an existing client.

• The best service providers keep their customers nearly 50% longer than their competitors.

4. It yields better bottom-line results.

There's a host of ways in which great service will effectively contribute positively to the bottom line at your company. Most are very directly linked to financial results. Service effectiveness can directly increase sales. It brings repeat business. It reduces errors and waste. It builds customer loyalty. It reduces the amount of time managers have to spend fixing problems.

5. It makes for a better place to work.

If you raise service standards in your organization, you're almost guaranteed to produce a more enjoyable workplace. When you and your staff are focused on giving to those around you, on being courteous, on going the extra mile for your customers, then that spirit can't help but carry over into the way that we all work with each other. I've learned the hard way that more than any benefits program, bonus system, or retirement plan we can put in place, the way people treat their peers is really one of the biggest contributors to quality of workplace. This has obvious advantages for us as leaders: less time spent mediating disputes between staff members who really don't want resolution, less stress for us personally, and hence fewer headaches to take home to inflict on our families. All of which means we have more time to spend on things that contribute positively to our lives.

6. It helps you attract better people to work with you.

As it becomes increasingly difficult to hire enough people to do the work that needs to be done, a more enjoyable workplace may be the selling tool we need to attract the best employees out there. Like prospective customers, the people we want to hire are choosing between us and some other employment options. As good service providers, we have two advantages in this area. First, the positive nature of our work environment gives us an immediate edge—good people want to work in a good place.

Second, I know that the more we give great service, the more likely we are to attract and hire service-oriented staff. We all want to be in a setting where we believe we'll be working with like-minded people. So where do service-oriented people want to work? In businesses that already give good service!

7. It's easier.

This is a benefit that's usually recognized only by long-time service givers. Newer staff members, on the other hand, rarely get it; they're still operating in the more orthodox mindset that says that giving great service is more work. Over 20 years in service have taught me that the opposite is true; it almost always ends up being easier to do things well and make the customer's experience something special than it is to do a slipshod job and clean up the mess later. Long-time service providers know this intuitively because they've expended energy handling complaints, replacing inaccurately delivered product, dealing with budget shortages, and calming unhappy customers. They're all too aware that, in the end, it takes more time, money, and energy to fix things that simply could have been taken care of up front.

8. It's the right thing to do.

On a less practical and far more spiritual level, I think that giving great service is just the right thing to do. Whatever one's ethnic or religious background, pretty much everyone in the world acknowledges that giving is the way to go. I firmly believe that when we're giving great service to our guests, we are making some small, positive contribution to their lives. We leave them smiling. We send them home with a new flavor experience. We give them a nice service story to share with their friends, neighbors, and their children. Does great service from Zingerman's solve all their problems? No. Does it resolve the struggles of the world? No way. But it does add something positive to what is generally a stressful society. And I think that's a nice thing to do. I know that some will say this sounds incredibly naïve, but just think of what would happen to the world if everyone was focused on how they could provide great service to others, instead of thinking first about what they have coming to themselves.

"Make a ritual of pausing frequently to appreciate and be thankful...Notice that the more you become a connoisseur of gratitude, the less you are the victim of resentment, depression and despair. Gratitude will act as an elixir that will gradually dissolve the hard shell of your ego—your need to possess and control—transforming you into a generous being. The sense of gratitude produces true spiritual alchemy, makes us magnanimous—large souled."
—Sam Keen, *Hymns to an Unknown God*

why is great service hard to find?

In all your years in management, have you ever had anyone tell you that good service was a waste of time? I don't think I have. Have you ever interviewed a candidate for a job who told you that they thought giving great customer service was stupid? Pretty much everyone you talk to today is theoretically in favor of giving good service. Even folks in Washington are on the service bandwagon; politicians and statisticians are all telling us how our future success will come in the form of a service economy. So then let me ask the only slightly less-than-obvious question: If everyone's so in favor of giving great service, how come it's so darned hard to find?

Over the years, we've come up with a wealth of very real reasons why this theoretical darling of the business world is in such short supply in real life.

1. It's unfamiliar.

For openers, I think that superior service is hard to find because, quite simply, we don't grow up with it. I don't know about you, but I don't have any childhood memories of traveling around town with my mother and having her point out examples of sterling service. I mean, I recall her talking about education and how important it was to be an upstanding citizen, but I don't remember a darned thing about service ever coming up.

So what's the big deal? Well, since I spend so much time in the kitchen, let me put it into a cooking context. Although I love it now, as a kid I paid little attention to food. Mostly we ate things like hamburgers, meatloaf, some steak, Kraft macaroni and cheese, and fish sticks. But every Friday night my grandmother used to prepare a traditional Jewish Sabbath meal which always started with chopped liver. Now, I was hardly hovering in the kitchen checking out her technique. When I arrived in Ann Arbor in 1974 to start school, I had little idea of the basics of cooking. But I'm pretty sure that if you had given me a recipe for chopped liver and the necessary ingredients, I'd have been able to make it come out pretty close to the way chopped liver should be. Even though

I didn't really know how to cook, I knew how the liver should look, what its texture should be, and how it should taste. I'd unconsciously internalized the essence of good chopped liver. And I'm pretty confident I'd have been able to create a reasonable facsimile.

On the other hand, if you'd given me a recipe for gumbo (now one of my favorite dishes), I'd never have gotten close to making anything resembling a good one. Although I'm sure I'd heard the word, I had no idea what a gumbo was, what it looked like, how thick or thin it ought to be, or how it should taste. Who knows what I'd have cooked up. And I think the same idea applies to service. It's hard to get something to come out right when you have no real, internalized sense of what it's supposed to be like when it's going well. Great service? Sure, everyone's all for it. But the truth of the matter is that hardly anyone really knows what it looks like, which means that without clear expectations and effective training, most of our staffers are out on the frontlines of life making a mess of our promise to provide great service to our guests.

2. It's not respected.

Although our systems pay homage to service, American culture actually looks down on the people who provide it. Although everyone says they want to get great service, far fewer want to actually give it. The truth is that if you're a service provider, it's more than likely that you're considered by at least part of your peer group as something of a "failure." Successful people simply aren't supposed to end up working in service jobs. Those are roles for teenagers on their way to other, more "meaningful," careers.

When I was still a young kid, my grandparents sold their laundry business and went into real estate. The end to their work as service providers was something they celebrated; they'd worked hard so that their children and grandchildren (like me, the oldest) wouldn't get stuck in such a hard-service spot again. By helping to send all of us to college they did their part, and ended up with a couple doctors, a lawyer, and a successful psychologist. But somehow here I am, back smack-dab in the middle of the service world. The difference, though, is that unlike my grandparents, I never feel that I'm stuck with service. I choose it. I embrace it. In fact, I actually like it.

3. It requires more work in the moment.

In an era when the American dream seems to run along the lines of, "get as much as possible for as little effort as you have to give," great service doesn't stand much chance on its own. And although we truly believe that it's rewarding and actually easier in the long run—both emotionally and financially—the reality of day-to-day work life is that if you're not ready to work your butt off in the interest of making great service a reality, it's just not going to happen.

4. It's hard to get John Wayne out of the way.

The behavior required to provide great service often runs counter to the entire image of strength and success we project in this country. Think about it: What do we tell people it means to be "strong"? You stand up for what you believe. You fight for what's fair. You don't take guff from bullies. All of that is well and good on the street, but when it comes to service, every one of those things is likely to get us into big trouble. Great service is almost the exact opposite of what we've been taught: To give it we have to be ready and able to back down, and then back down some more. We have to back down even when customers are clearly in the wrong. And if customers come out and tell us that we're not giving good service while we're backing down, then we have to back down even more.

Even if one believes in giving great service, the truth is that when we hire someone they've already been internalizing this "fight for your rights" mentality for 20, 30, or 40 years, and there's just no quick way to override that socialization. To the contrary, most people have processed it so well that even those of us who've intellectually chosen to be great service providers can still quickly lapse into "standing up" to the unreasonable customer if we're not careful. Why? What do we all do when we're under enormous pressure? We go back to the behaviors that we're most comfortable with, the ones that we're the most accustomed to. And let me tell you, that rarely means giving great service.

5. It's not fair.

Here's one theory that's so true it always gets a chuckle when I talk about it. It goes like this: Great service is hard to find because, quite simply, it isn't fair. And unfortunately, we're all raised with the notion that life is supposed to be fair. I know that I regularly complained to my parents that this, that, or the other thing "wasn't fair." "Mickey got to go to the movies..." "Laurie didn't have to stay home to clean her room..." I don't think I've ever met a single American who couldn't relate to having said or heard that sort of thing way too much growing up.

Sadly, service simply is not fair. Never has been, never will be. Sometimes I'm really nice to a customer and they're mean to me. Quite often I go out of my way for a guest and they don't appreciate my efforts at all. Sometimes considerate customers get less attention than the ones who make our lives difficult by complaining about almost everything we do. None of this is fair. Not fair at all.

To combat this predilection for "fairness," I've started to tell our staff that, "'Fair' is another planet. And we, unfortunately, are not on it. If you need things to be fair," I explain, "then it's time to think about a different place to work. You might consider trading this job for a career in jurisprudence, where, I assume, that sort of 'fairness' is the first priority. But in the service world, 'fair' is...well, it's another planet."

6. There's plenty of good talk, but also bad walk.

A lot of leadership people don't like to hear it, but our experience is that employees will never treat customers any better than their leaders do. All too often, service suffers because leadership folks don't walk their service talk. I mean, it's not fair (just wanted to see if you were paying attention), but the staff will go by what we do, not what we say. And when we walk past a customer who hasn't been helped without acknowledging them, we're sending a really clear message: "It's OK not to wait on customers when you have more important things to do." When we sit in managers' meetings and refuse requests from the staff to assist with guest service, we send an equally clear message: "Meetings are more important than customer service." We also send the message that if you move up in the organization, then service is less important. Quite simply, this is completely backwards.

If service is as important as we say it is, then we at the "top" have to be more committed to giving great service. We have to be more aggressive about making it happen. And we have to really do it, not just talk about it!

7. Reward systems don't reinforce it.

If you really look at what goes on in the workplace, you'll find that all too often there's actually very little reward for giving great service. The folks who go out of their way to provide great service to guests get little or no recognition from us as leaders. Frequently, we fail to notice; we forget to comment. And more often than not, great service-givers get pretty much the same compensation as everyone else. If your reward systems—both the formal ones, like pay rates and bonuses; and the informal ones, like the small comments and pats on the back—don't reinforce your commitment to great service, it's unlikely that you're going to get it.

8. It's not defined.

Probably the biggest reason of all, though, is that most organizations fail to really define what great service is. They want it. They ask people to deliver it. They even promise it to their clients. The staff means well and they want to come through for the company and for the customers. But when you ask around at most organizations, you'll find that no one really agrees on exactly what it is they're supposed to deliver. And if you don't know the rules of the service game you're playing, it doesn't really matter how much you care or how hard you try—you aren't going to succeed.

If we want our staff to win the game of great service, we have to teach them how to play. We have to define great service for them if we want them to have a chance to deliver it.

defining it

zingerman's recipe for successful service

"We are ultimately at home in the world not through dominating or explaining or appreciating, but through caring and being cared for."
Milton Mayeroff,
On Caring

The vision of service success that we have here at Zingerman's isn't long and complicated. In fact, it's actually quite simple and, I think, inspiring. Our vision is that we consistently give great service to all of our customers in every element of our work; that we give great service to each other as peers; and that we provide great service to our community. More specifically, we define it very clearly and concretely by using our "3 Steps to Great Service" and our "5 Steps to Handling Customer Complaints." Our vision is that by the end of his or her first week, any new staffer will be able to tell you what he or she is authorized to do to make a customer happy. (In a few pages, you'll know too.) And, our vision is that everyone who's worked with us for 60 days can easily tell you, and perform, those same three and five steps.

recipe from:
Zingerman's ®

3 steps to great service

 Ingredients:

- An inspiring, strategically sound, and clearly documented vision for great service
- Strong, service-oriented leadership
- Clear and well-communicated expectations
- Good training to share those expectations and to let people practice
- Giving staff the authorization to take action to make great service a reality
- Positive recognition and reward for great service-givers

Procedure:

1. Figure out what the customer wants.
2. Get it for them, accurately, politely, and enthusiastically.
3. Go the extra mile for the customer.

Procedure for Making the "3 Steps" a Reality

As you read through the "3 Steps to Great Service," you may find yourself thinking, "What's the big deal? I already do all of that." If that's the case, you surely aren't alone. Many leaders in service-oriented organizations intuitively do this stuff. But the problem in most organizations is not that you or I don't know  how to give great service, it's that we aren't the ones waiting on most of our customers—our staff is. And for most staff members, the stuff that's in the "3 Steps" is not obvious, it's not intuitive, and, in all too many instances, it's not happening.

Step 1: Figure out what the customer wants.

If you don't know what your customer is looking for, what are your chances of getting it for them? Slim at best, I'd say. So if you want to have a shot at this thing, you've got to get going by getting a handle on what your customer wants. Of course, this sounds easier than it often is. Customers frequently fail to express their needs clearly. Many times customers don't even know what they want. More challenging still are customers who think they know what they want but actually want something else.

You start this work by doing what we call "engaging the guest." That means you talk to them—a lot! (You can substitute "write to them," if you're working online.) In this context, we define the term "engage" to mean that we spend as much time with the customer as we possibly can. The more we talk to them, the more we'll learn about who they are, what they do, how they use our product, what their hopes and fears are.

What's so hard about this? Nothing, really. It's just that the average service person in this country begins customer interactions with the intention of spending as little time talking to them as they have to. Now, if what the customer wants is speed and little else,

10-4 rule

One guideline we teach that's helped to clarify service expectations is what we call the "10-4 Rule." I can't remember who I learned it from, but whoever you were, thanks for sharing it. It works! The rule says that anytime you come within ten feet of a guest you make solid eye contact. And when you get within four feet, you greet them verbally.

The 10-4 Rule is great. It's clear, simple, and easy to remember. I'm particularly fond of it because it helps us to avoid one of my service pet peeves, something I've come to call the "Ostrich Syndrome." We've all seen it at the airport or in some other bureaucratic "service" setting: There's a long line of customers waiting to be served, and although there are ten staffers standing behind their computers, only one "window" is open. The other nine folks just keep staring intensely at their screens and will not look at their customers for anything. It always seems as if they're sure that if they just keep looking down long enough, the customers will go away. The funny thing is that while they're wrong in the moment, in the long run, it's a self-fulfilling prophecy—ignore your customers long enough and they will surely shop somewhere else!

you're in good shape using that approach. But in our business and in many others, life is much more complex than that. To really have a shot at successfully giving great service, you've usually got to go deeper than the typical, "Can I help you?"

The next part of finding out what the guest wants involves listening to his or her response. Tune in to the details, the unspoken stuff that will help you better identify your customer's needs. Learn to read between the lines: Note his or her demeanor (happy? angry? tired?), and companions (family? out-of-town guests?), tone of voice (confident? concerned?), and so on. All of these details will help you determine what the customer would like you to do. Listen closely, like you're on a first date and you really want to make a positive, lasting impression. In fact, when you get good at it, you'll be able to identify products and services your customer wants but didn't even know existed.

Whatever you do, please don't ever make assumptions in service settings. If you don't already know the ASSUME saying, you will—shortly after you assume that you know what customers mean or want. When you have even the slightest hesitation that something isn't clear, always, always, ask for clarification. Always read back orders, or repeat back the guest's requests, to make sure you have understood the customer correctly.

Step 2: Get it for them.

This second step also sounds simple, but it's difficult to do. It requires real concentration,

"Good service 'takes the extra step,' 'goes out of its way,' shows imaginative variations, finds precise ways of pleasing. It calls on imagination and delights the imagination as well as the senses."
—James Hillman, *Kinds of Power*

focus, and a commitment to getting things done right. We break this second step down into three facets:

A. Do it accurately. In other words, to state the obvious, if the customer asked for a quarter-pound, give them a quarter-pound. In my experience, this is the area in which using well-designed systems—consistently and intelligently—will significantly increase the likelihood of successfully delivering service accurately. Double-checking orders, order forms that walk staffers through the appropriate questions, realistic time frames for production targets, etc.—all will contribute to improved accuracy. (For more on this, see p. 48 on our "4 Steps to Order Accuracy.") As we tell our staff, "You can't eat good intentions for dinner."

B. Do it politely. Politeness really does make a big difference in the service world. All those words our parents taught us to use, like "please" and "thank you," go a long way toward making a customer feel like he or she received good service. Now, I'm not saying that "please" and "thank you" will make you a better human being. In truth, how you talk to your friends and family outside of the workplace is up to you. But in a service setting, courtesy counts. So whatever work our staff might be engaged in, we ask them to do it politely.

C. Do it enthusiastically. I learned the importance of this third facet courtesy of some helpful staffers who taught me that you can consistently say the words "please" and "thank you," but still make it clear that you don't really mean it. (Over the years, you've probably worked with a few people who do this.) What we mean here by "do it enthusiastically," is that we want each customer we wait on to leave their interaction feeling as though they were the best thing that happened to us that day.

When I present this material in person, I always pause to let this message sink in. Within 30 seconds, someone in the room inevitably starts to roll their eyes and give me that "you've-got-to-be-kidding" look. So, trying to be as direct and to-the-point as possible, I reiterate my expectation by stating very seriously, "I'm not kidding. We want each guest to leave their interaction with you feeling as though they were the best thing that happened to you that day. If you're not sure that you've convinced them of this, then be more enthusiastic."

Now, it may have already dawned on you that it's absolutely impossible for every customer you wait on to be the best thing that happened to you that day. You're correct. But I didn't say I expected each customer to actually be the best thing that happened to you—only that I wanted them to leave thinking that they were. The former is impossible, but the latter, while difficult, is definitely do-able.

What this often comes down to, if you think it through, is acting. None of us are eternally in good moods, nor do we love every customer. Sometimes I'm tired, downright exhausted. Sometimes the last thing in the world I want to do is wait on another customer. Sometimes I want to run away and hide. But all of those are my problems, not our customers'. And in order to deliver great service to our guests, I need to keep it that way by acting enthusiastic and upbeat anyway.

"But," someone will always complain, "that's not honest."

And they're absolutely right. It's not honest. But I remind them that our customers aren't paying us to be honest. They're paying us to get a great experience, a key component of which is great service. They come to us for great corned beef, consulting or catering. If they want honesty, they pay their therapist.

Now, I'm not saying that you should lie to your customers, nor am I suggesting that people who hate giving service are likely to make good service providers if they're reasonably good actors. I'm saying that it's imperative in the service world to be able to act like you mean it, even though at any given moment, you may not. When you go to the theater to see a play, do you really care if the lead actor is in a good mood? Do you care if the actor and actress are mad at each other? Are you concerned about whether or not the lead actress is bored with her role? I'm not. I just want to see a good show. I paid my admission fee, and I want to see good theater.

When our customers come to us, they want to see a good show too. Since that's what they expect, it's our responsibility to deliver it. We don't have a sign up on the wall that says, "Ari's first day making sandwiches, 20% off!" We don't post notices that say things like, "Short-staffed today, everything in the store 25% off while we're rude." In fact, we charge the same price whether we're short-staffed, tired, under-trained, crabby or any of the hundreds of other reasonable things that happen to us that can get in the way of delivering great service. In the acting world, at the end of the day it doesn't really matter whether the actors actually feel the emotions they're portraying. Rather, the big question is, "What does it look like to the audience?" Whether or not you really mean it, you have to convince the audience—in this case, our customers—that you feel enthusiastic. Your challenge in giving great service is to get every single customer you wait on to leave feeling as though they were the best thing that happened to you that day.

Step 3: Go the extra mile!

In most service settings, these first two steps as out-

can you be too enthusiastic?

Many times, when I give presentations on service to our staff and I get to the part about enthusiasm, someone will caution me that, "some customers don't want you to be enthusiastic." I acknowledge quickly that they're right. I know that some guests don't want enthusiasm—they're not in a good mood and, in their case, being enthusiastic is inappropriate. (Actually, this is just going back to "Step 1"—Figure out what the customer wants. If they want quick and dour, give them quick and dour.) That said, these people are the exception, not the rule. And, as I regularly tell anyone who asks, for over 20 years I've maybe had two complaints about staffers being "too enthusiastic." Then I challenge the staff: If I get a Code Red (see page 63) documenting a customer complaint that a staffer was too enthusiastic, I'll buy that staffer lunch.

lined above would add up to an exceptional customer experience. If the business you were buying from figured out what you wanted and then got it for you—accurately, politely and enthusiastically—you'd probably be pretty pleased. But the way we see it here, these first two steps are the bare minimum we can get away with. To do less, we believe, would be ripping off our customers. To give great service, we have to do the third step, what we call "going the extra mile."

Going the extra mile at Zingerman's means doing more than the guest has asked for—actually exceeding their expectations. Going the extra mile makes our customers leave their interactions with us thinking, "Wow! That was really nice." And, we know from experience, it makes an enormous difference in the quality of the customer's experience.

There are countless things we can do in the food business to go the extra mile for our customers. At Zingerman's, they might include:

- Giving a taste of a new item to a regular customer.

- Sending an article to a client about their field of work.

- Calling a customer back a few days after they received their order to follow up on the effectiveness of the work we did for them.

- Adding a sample of something extra to an order.
- Sending a hand-written "thank you" note or email to a customer.
- Carrying a customer's bag to their car.

This is all simple stuff. Physically, it's usually the easiest part of the process. But because we—not the customer—have to come up with what it means to go the extra mile for the guest, it's often the most challenging part of the process, mentally. If the guest asks for something, simply filling their request does not qualify as an extra mile.

Ultimately, I think these extra miles bring that little something extra to our service. It's the stuff that sets us apart from our countless competitors and that keeps our customers coming back for more positive Zingerman's Experiences.

zingerman's
4 steps to order accuracy

We use these now in almost every element of our work, from packing sandwich orders to sending out consulting proposals. In case we ever doubt that they work, we have only to ignore them once or twice to be reminded, because we inevitably end up making mistakes.

1. Read Back

Every order should be repeated back to the guest to catch any number of honest mistakes that can be caused by the inevitable distractions, different terminology, and so on.

2. Precheck

After the person who took the order completes Step 1 by reading the order back, the written order is then checked for accuracy and physically signed-off on by someone other than the order taker. This second set of eyes will often catch something missed by the original service person in the heat of the moment—an out-of-stock product, missing information, an entry that isn't quite clear, and more.

3. Recheck

After being produced and packed—but before being delivered—the order is inspected and signed by someone other than the person producing it. Again, this additional set of eyes is imperative. In the same way that the person who proofs this book before it goes to print has a much better chance of catching small typos than I ever will having written it over the last two years, a person who didn't pack the actual order is far more likely to catch a small error than the person who packed it.

4. Confirm Upon Delivery

When the order is delivered to the customer we need to verbally review what we've brought them and then confirm it with the recipient—item by item if possible—before they sign for it. This allows for one last check to make sure that we've correctly heard what the guest would like and accurately filled it (per our "3 Steps to Great Service").

Code Greens—how we catch 'em doing it right

As easy as it is for most of us in leadership to fixate on what's going wrong, we would benefit from recognizing the countless things that are already being done well. At Zingerman's, we actually spread the responsibility for identifying successes throughout our entire organization. Toward that end, we've created what we call a "Code Green." It's an easy-to-use, one page form that allows anyone in the organization that hears a customer compliment—on service, product quality or anything else—to document it.

I like the Code Green form a lot, because:

It helps recognize people in the organization who are doing great work. Using the Code Green means that there's a quick and easy way for us to "share the wealth" when one of us hears a customer compliment on an everyday product or service.

The forms get positive feedback to the people who actually produce what we sell. Although the people who work in positions with high customer interactivity may regularly hear compliments about our food, those who actually make it often go weeks, months, or even years without anyone letting them know how great their product is. You'd be amazed how much the smallest compliment can mean to some of these folks.

It focuses attention on some of the many success stories that happen, literally almost every minute, in our work. It spreads the power of recognition throughout the organization. Code Greens aren't just for managers to fill out. Anyone who hears a compliment is expected to write one up, which means that each of us has the power to spread positive energy and become a respected leader in the company. The simple use of the form also helps to spread the practice—instead of just the theory—of empowerment throughout our organization. If you think that we aren't being positive enough in our leadership work, then simply grab a stack of these forms, pass them out to your peers, fill 'em out and start making a positive difference.

Sharing success stories is one of the best ways to teach service techniques. You can talk concepts 'til kingdom come, but some staff members just won't get it until you can give them a concrete, hands-on example of what you're talking about. So share the stories and watch the successes multiply. Please visit http://info.zingtrain.com/greatservice to get a copy of our Code Green form.

zingerman's 5 steps to handling customer complaints

If you've been in the service world for more than a couple of days, you've almost certainly had an opportunity to learn about this challenging subject. Intellectually, we all understand its importance; everyone knows that the better we manage a customer complaint, the more likely we are to keep a valued customer. And yet, the businesses that handle customer complaints consistently well are few and far between.

I'll tell you right now, it's hardly my favorite part of my job. In fact, I don't think I've met too many people who work in the service world who look forward to dealing with customer complaints; my informal statistics have shown me that there are a couple of people out of every 100 or so who actually enjoy it. I'm not one of them. I don't like it now, and I never really have. Complaints often leave me feeling down—at times even devastated—for days. I take our customer service very seriously, and when we fall short, I have a hard time rationalizing it away. In fact, I don't want to. The day I start writing off unhappy customers as "unimportant," or treating them as insignificant statistics, is the day I'll get out of the service industry.

In his excellent book, *The Science of Shopping*, Paco Underhill writes that: "Retailers must accept that there are no new customers—the population isn't booming, and we already have more stores than we need."

If you're running a kiosk at an airport where you have a captive audience, then maybe customer retention isn't something you worry about. But around here, we need all the customers we can get. So when one of our customers complains, there's no question that we're going to do pretty much anything and everything we have to do to keep them as a client.

We've found that the best way to keep complaining customers coming back is to follow these five simple-to-say, but hard-to-do, steps. I've taught these steps in our own organization and all over the country for many years now. And in my experience, they work well in nearly any industry and in almost any setting, whether it's retail or wholesale, on the phone or in person.

here's how we do it at zingerman's:

Step 1: Acknowledge the customer's complaint.

If a customer has taken the time and effort to let us know that they're unhappy with the product or service they've purchased, they're looking for us to let them know that their concerns have been heard. So our first step to effective complaint handling is to simply let them know that we have indeed heard what they have to say.

We do this with a simple one- or two-word response like, "Wow." Or maybe, "Oh." If the complaint is big, you can use the two in tandem, as in, "Oh, wow!" If you want to *recipe from:*

Zingerman's ®

5 steps to effectively handling customer complaints

 Ingredients:

- An inspiring, strategically sound, and clearly documented vision for great service
- Strong, service-oriented leadership
- Clear and well-communicated expectations
- Good training to share those expectations and to let people practice
- Giving staff the authorization to take action to make great service a reality
- Positive recognition and reward for great service-givers

Procedure:

1. Acknowledge the customer's complaint.
2. Sincerely apologize.
3. Take action to make things right.
4. Thank the customer.
5. Write it up.

be more verbose, you can try, "I can certainly see why you're upset." It's that simple, really. Just let 'em know you heard what they said.

The importance of this acknowledgment may be obvious to you if you've been at this stuff for a long time. But in my experience, it's incredible how rarely service people do it. In fact, service providers will often do anything but acknowledge that they've heard the complaint.

To take this acknowledgment issue one step further, note that non-verbal messages can sometimes say as much or even more to a customer as the words we use. Folded arms, staring at the floor, or looking like you can't wait to run away won't cut it. I make sure to convey concern through my tone of voice and body language— gentle eye contact, head-nodding and a caring tone of voice work well.

Step 2: Sincerely apologize.

Once you've acknowledged that you've heard the customer's concerns, your next challenge is to apologize. Simply and sincerely, with no excuses, no explanations, no badgering, and no sending them off to see someone in "customer service." Just something along the lines of, "I'm very sorry about that" or, "I'm so sorry that this happened" or, "I'm sorry you were so frustrated." There are a million ways to say it, but the point is that you sincerely express regret.

Any staff member can follow these first two steps. They don't need to know anything about what you do other than to be familiar with, and willing, to adhere to the first part of this recipe. They don't have to know your products. They don't have to know what to do to fix the problem. All they have to do is listen attentively to what the customer is saying. Most customers are so used to hearing defensiveness and dumb excuses that they're almost taken by surprise when they hear acknowledgment and apology. And when they do, their tension level inevitably drops, making them much easier to deal with. Which, in turn, reduces staff stress levels and improves job satisfaction, thus increasing the quality of your service.

Pay attention as you travel around your town and you'll be amazed at how unbelievably rare it is for a service person to respond to a complaint in this manner. What do most service staff do? Take your pick from the following list of things customers hear all too often:

- "You're gonna have to go talk to the manager. There's nothing I can do."
- "You're wrong."
- "You didn't order that. You're gonna have to pay an extra charge now if you want me to change it for you."
- "Our sandwich maker is new today."
- "We're really short-staffed this morning."
- "I can't help that. You should have..."

And don't forget the classic:

- "I told the manager this was gonna happen."

Or my all-time favorite:

- "Oh, that happens all the time."

exceptions to the "don't explain" rule

There are a few situations where it is actually OK to explain to a customer why things went wrong. This would be when we've got a guest who is truly interested in the inner workings of our organization, an individual who sincerely wants to understand how things could have happened the way they did. When you've got one of these folks in front of you, by all means take the time to "tour" them through the business and help them understand what happened. This interested minority will feel like they're getting exceptional service—we're meeting their need by providing them with a thoughtful, non-defensive explanation of how things went awry.

As a caveat though, I will say that the people who truly want to be told why and how their order was messed up are few and very far between. Most customers really aren't interested in why something happened. They just want us to make things right so that they can be on their way.

The truth of the matter is that it's totally normal to think any or all of the above. Often these "excuses" are actually accurate assessments of what went wrong. Customers frequently do make mistakes when they order; sometimes we really are short-staffed; some days we really do have a new trainee making sandwiches. But the one thing that all of these excuses have in common is that they are our problems, not our customers'. Effective service providers don't deal in excuses; they take responsibility for fixing things. Sure, you may be short-staffed, but generally consumers could care less. They just want what they ordered. So when you catch yourself wanting to explain, just swallow, take a deep breath, and go back to the beginning by starting out with "Step 1," an acknowledgment that you've heard what they said, and "Step 2," a sincere apology. Then move on to the next step.

Step 3: Take action to make things right.

If you've gotten off on the right foot by following "Steps 1" and "2" (acknowledging and apologizing), then it's probably time to move on to "Step 3" and do something to make things right for your customer.

What would that be? Well, sometimes it's surprisingly straightforward. They weren't happy with the product? Replace it. Delivery was late? Refund their delivery charge. Other times it's more complex. Different people want different things. What's likely to make one man happy may fall far short of what you need to do for his next-door neighbor. Or much more than you need to do for his father-in-law. How do you know what to do to make things right for the guest? The best way is simply to ask them: "Wow. I'm really sorry. What can I do to make this right for you?"

Amazingly, most customers will just come right out and tell you. And even more amazingly, in many cases, what they want will be far less than what you were prepared to offer.

At Zingerman's, we authorize our staff to do whatever they think needs to be done to make a dissatisfied guest happy. You read that right. They're authorized to do whatever they need to do to make things right for the customer: Refund money. Replace product. Deliver a new order. Get a manager or partner to help. Or even all of the above.

go back to steps 1&2
do not pass go
do not collect $200

In the case of a really irate customer, you may need to repeat "Step 1" and "Step 2" over and over again before they're ready to let you move on to resolution. We once had a very diligent manager, Claude, at the Deli who'd attended all of our service training; he knew our steps to handling a complaint backwards and forwardss In theory, he was ready for almost anything.

One evening, Claude was called over by a concerned staffer to respond to a guest who was extremely unhappy with their meal. He handled it by the book: he acknowledged the problem, he apologized, and then he asked them what he could do to make things right for them. Unfortunately, the customer was so unhappy he wasn't ready to move to resolution. Although the customer had paused in his presentation of the issues, he wasn't really finished complaining. Claude, on the other hand, was—understandably—eager to get things wrapped up. Together they were on a complaint collision course: The customer kept complaining, and Claude began to practically demand to know how he could make things right. In truth, I'm sure he was ready to do just about anything the customer would have wanted. But he was too far out in front of the customer in the process, ready to resolve it while the guest was still intent on venting.

What this customer needed was for Claude to just keep on acknowledging and apologizing over and over until the guest had cooled down. Lots of empathy, plenty of patience, a lot of good listening and everything would have worked out fine. But in his eagerness to get to an answer, Claude had long since stopped listening. And the result was poor service instead of a well-handled complaint.

Why would we want front-line staff to take care of things?

For starters, it's easier for the customer. They don't have to wait. They don't have to repeat their story for a second (or third or fourth) time. It's also easier for the employee. And, more importantly, it helps our staff to feel like they're not just there to take flak—they're actually empowered to fix.

What if the staff person doesn't know what to do?

That's a likely reality. Sometimes the staff member is in over their head or hasn't yet been trained to deal with the complexities of a given problem. In other instances, the guest isn't just upset, they're irate, and a front-line staffer might need backup. Sometimes what the customer wants is to talk to a manager. At other times, the situation simply isn't very clear, and it takes someone with a lot of experience to sort it out. In any of those situations, we simply ask our staffers to go through "Step 1" (acknowledging the guest's complaint) and "Step 2" (apologizing). And then we ask them to simply tell the customer that they'd like to go get a manager to take care of them. Of course, managers need to be trained to deal with these more ambiguous, high-anxiety situations. If ours aren't comfortable handling things, we ask them to again acknowledge the problem and apologize, then go get more help, usually by bringing in one of the partners. By the time we're done, the organization—the front-line staff person, a manager, a partner, or, in some cases, all three in tandem—is taking an unpleasant situation and making it right for the customer in question.

Does the staff ever go overboard?

Sure, every once in a while that's
what happens. We do ask the staff
to be reasonable—giving $1,000 to
someone who didn't like their
brownie is obviously out of hand.
But you know what? In all our
years of doing this, I don't think anything that extreme
has ever happened. In fact, it's very safe to say that new
employees here at Zingerman's almost never do too
much; they actually consistently err on the side of not
doing enough. And if they do give away more than they
should? Well, I figure that it's a small price to pay to keep
customers coming back.

Don't some customers take advantage of our willingness
to do whatever it takes?

Probably. But in my experience, there are only a very few
exceptional customers who act dishonestly. And rather
than punish the 99% of our customers who are totally
honest in an effort to protect ourselves from the 1%
who try to pull something over on us, we accept that on
occasion we're going to get taken advantage of. In my
mind, it's worth the risk in order to avoid offending all
those great customers who are totally on-the-level. I'm
sure some people will argue that we get away with this
because we're in a smallish town in the Midwest. Maybe—
I've never done business anyplace else. But I still believe
this is the right way to go.

The main point here, though, isn't that we authorize our staff to do whatever it takes. Depending on the industry in which you're working—health care, for example—it's certainly reasonable to set narrower boundaries than ours. The key is that the staff needs to be clear on what those boundaries are so that they know what they are or are not authorized to do.

What about the customers who you "just can't make happy"?

I believe that if we really work at it, if we really put our heads together and think and act creatively, there's almost always a way to take a customer complaint and turn it into a positive experience. Certainly, in difficult situations, front-line staff may be hard-pressed to pull it off. So in our organization we ask people to keep passing the complaint "up" the organizational chart until it gets taken care of. A front-line staff member who's in over his head can call the supervisor for help, who, in turn, may get a manager, who, when stumped, may call a partner. At Zingerman's, only partners are authorized to decide that we don't want someone as our customer. During all our years in business, I think there's been about eight. Not too many when you think of all the thousands of difficult customer situations we've had to handle.

Step 4: Thank the customer.

Although they're discouraging to hear, complaints from our guests really do offer us a critical opportunity to improve our performance. We appreciate that our customers let us know where we've gone astray. So when we've successfully navigated our way through the first three steps I've outlined, we express our appreciation by sincerely thanking our customers for letting us know that they were upset.

Statistics say that for every customer who complains, there are nine or ten others who were just as unhappy but said nothing. (I don't have any trouble believing this, since I almost never complain when I'm an unhappy customer.) This silent majority often voices its concerns using what we call "economic criticism." That's what happens when the customer takes his or her money and spends it at one of the other 1,500 places within ten miles of us that's vying for food dollars. A customer who cares enough to complain is providing us with a valuable opportunity to make things right.

What happens when you don't handle a complaint effectively? The data I've seen says that every unhappy customer will likely tell at least ten (some say 20, some say 30) friends about their bad experience—if we start losing customers that way, pretty soon we won't have anyone coming in.

To compound the seriousness of the situation, add this fact to the mix: Perhaps 80% or 90% of customers who complain are more unhappy after their complaint has been handled than they were before they spoke up! I used to question the validity of these numbers, but listening to attendees at our seminars recall their nightmarish customer service experiences around the country, I have to say I believe it. Sadly, that's an awful lot of unhappy customers out there circulating horror stories about well-meaning businesses.

On the other hand, the effort involved in handling a complaint properly ensures that no matter what we have to do, the guest will leave feeling satisfied. Our average customer comes to see us a couple of times a week. I figure that they spend, conservatively, $10 a visit. In a college town like Ann Arbor, where almost everyone is seemingly leaving for another city or school at some point, our average customer lives here for about five years. $20 a week is about $1000 a year, and over five years, that means that each individual will spend about $5000 with us. (And that doesn't even take into account the cost of all the negative publicity they could pass along to friends and family.)

So how far should you go to keep a $5000 customer in a business of our size? Pretty darned far! We will go to almost any length to make sure that we do not lose a guest—there's absolutely no doubt in my mind that a well-handled complaint can turn an unhappy customer into a lifetime supporter.

Step 5: Write it up.

In order to effectively capture more data about what customers have to say, we document all the customer comments we can. We do this on what we call a "Code Red" form. I can say with confidence that the use of this form has been one of the best additions to our service systems over the years. It's easy to imagine that on a single day, seven or eight people at various spots in our orga-

nization might take a complaint from a single customer about the same item. One might come in at the Deli, a couple in Catering, more over the phone at Mail Order, and another over the Web. If we don't document each of those complaints and then compile and collate the data at one central point, none of the seven staffers would ever realize that the customer comment they'd handled was anything more than a small blip on a big service screen. Actually, seven or eight complaints about the same thing on a single day are an incredibly important issue that we need to address as quickly as possible.

What about mistakes we made that the customer didn't actually complain about?

The point is to gather meaningful data to improve our performance. If we realize that we've made a mistake but the customer only partially noticed, we ask our staff to just go ahead and write it up anyway. What's the risk? Remember, our goal is to catch any problems as early as we can, so we can make the Zingerman's Experience more rewarding for our customers and staff alike.

Who's responsible for documenting?

At Zingerman's, the individual who initially hears the complaint is responsible for writing it up within 24 hours. We choose to do it this way because we believe that the complaint "belongs" to whomever among us hears it first. If someone's not sure if he was the first to hear it, we 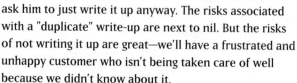 ask him to just write it up anyway. The risks associated with a "duplicate" write-up are next to nil. But the risks of not writing it up are great—we'll have a frustrated and unhappy customer who isn't being taken care of well because we didn't know about it.

Some folks in business argue that it's inappropriate for new front-line people to be writing up important problems or complaints. I take the opposite view. I believe it's our obligation as leaders to help them learn how to do this well. I'm confident that this method gets new staffers more involved in the organization. It makes a living example of our Guiding Principles by showing, first hand, that each of us can and will make a difference in the quality of service we provide. We also demonstrate that the quality of that service is really not contingent upon seniority, title, age, position, or anything else other than a willingness to take responsibility for the results of the work we all do.

On our Code Red form, we ask the person who handled the initial complaint to recommend "next steps" that should be taken in order to make things right for the customer. "Next steps" could include apology letters from managers or partners, the delivery of new product or additional information to the guest, a follow-up call a few weeks later to see if the quality is meeting the customer's expectations, and so on. The person who writes up the form can, and usually should, attach actual names to specific action steps. Then they must, of course, get copies of the form to everyone whose name is listed in the "actions needed" column.

At Zingerman's, the person who wrote up the form and the person they've identified as needing to take some "next steps" are each 100% responsible for making sure the actions are taken in a timely and effective manner. Again, this is regardless of hierarchical position in the organization, title, seniority, age or anything else. This means that it's quite possible that a 16-year-old busboy might be grabbing one of the managing partners by the arm and asking if they've sent the follow-up apology to Mrs. Aronoff. And you know what? I think that when interactions like that take place, it's a huge, huge success! It means that we've

"Good service comes from employees having a high degree of trust and respect for management and the company. Then and only then will good service come. You don't get good service from a system; you get it from an employee."

—Dave Longaberger, *The Longaberger Story: And How We Did It*

successfully built a sense of responsibility for service quality all the way through the organization.

Not only is this a positive result, I actually happen to think that it's probably more practical, too. The truth is, for that busboy, the customer complaint they need to follow-up on is likely a much more memorable part of their daily work than it is for a partner. For the busboy, this is a big issue—it's his customer and if we've successfully gotten across to him how important that customer is, then he's going to take it very seriously. And since he probably has only a single Code Red to follow up on, the likelihood that he'll remember to do so may actually be higher than it would be for the highly responsible, but often overwhelmed, partners who are dealing with a million issues and problems every day.

By keeping documented copies of all the Code Reds, we give ourselves many good opportunities to review and improve service: We can look for trends, identify ongoing issues, and so on. It also gives us an easy way to go the extra mile. The simple act of pulling a Code Red out of the files six months after a regular customer complained, then calling or emailing them to see if they've been satisfied with the product or service in question during their recent visits, is the sort of extra mile interaction that could win you a customer for life. For a copy of our Code Red form, please visit http://info.zingtrain.com/greatservice.

Living it
making the recipe a reality

"We need to distinguish between the values and visions to which we give lip service and those that are truly the basis for our actions."—Sam Keen, *Hymns to an Unknown God*

giving great service to the staff

I've already mentioned that if we want our customers to receive great service, we as leaders have to set the tone by modeling that behavior. But I'll ratchet our challenge up another level by stating that not only do we need to give great service to our clients, we've also got to give great service to our staff.

We address this at length in our approach to management, which we call "Servant Leadership." The name comes from an outstanding book by the late Robert Greenleaf. He explains the concept in much greater detail and far more eloquently than I will here, but in a nutshell, it goes like this: The leader's job in any organization is to serve the people in the organization. Now, most folks who hear this for the first time nod their heads as if it were the most obvious thing in the world, but life in most companies is exactly the opposite. Whether the expectation is stated or not, in most workplaces, the staff is supposed to serve the boss. I think this is backwards.

As the CEO of the Zingerman's Community of Businesses, my major "clients" are the managing partners of our businesses. Their major "customers" are their managers. The managers, in turn, are there to provide service to the front-line staff. And the front-line staff? They serve the customers. What kind of service do I provide to our staff? I greet them enthusiastically. I open the door for them. I offer to get them coffee when I can. I carry a box of bread or a sack of potatoes. The point isn't that I'm a great guy. Rather, the major message is that, quite simply, the service our staff gives to our guests will never consistently be better than the service that we, as leaders, give to the staff.

giving great service to each other

In our Guiding Principles, we specifically address this issue by stating:

"We give great service to each other as well as to our guests.

"We provide the same level of service in our work with our peers as we do with our guests. We go the extra mile for each other. We are polite, supportive, considerate, superb listeners, working on the basis of mutual respect and care."

In other words, all of the steps to providing great service that I've written about above apply not only to the way that we deal with our guests, but also to the way that we deal with each other. It's important to us that everyone who is a part of Zingerman's is served by the business, and by each of us as members of the organization. We're committed to providing the best possible service to the best of our ability to everyone who works at Zingerman's.

In our orientation for new staff members, I specifically address this issue when I review our Guiding Principles. I tell the group that, quite frankly, it's a given that they aren't going to like all of the folks who are part of our organization. "But," I continue, "We're paying you to act like you do. So when you see someone coming down the hall, I expect you to greet that coworker as enthusiastically as you would your best friend."

To take this idea one step further, let me state that the "5 Steps to Handling Complaints" are equally important in this context as well. In this case, it's almost—but not quite—the same as it would be with paying customers. Realistically, there will always be situations where our staff members are asking for or complaining about something that they may not fully understand. It could be that (we believe) they've inaccurately assessed the situation. Perhaps they just don't agree with the way we do business. In any of these instances, there is room for a significant departure from the way we treat staff like customers and how we treat customers like customers.

With paying customers, we would act as if they're always right, even when they're actually wrong.
But with staff, this won't work. If, for example:
- The staff member's reality is way off base;
- Their behavior is unethical or inappropriate;
- You believe the organization is going to suffer if we actually did something that the staff member is demanding we do.

In these instances, we need to find some constructive, effective way to work things through to resolution, regardless. The key is to do this in a very courteous, respectful, service-oriented manner. And, while at times challenging, it's also eminently doable.

the 5-90-5 rule

The 5-90-5 rule goes like this: I start with the optimistic assumption that everyone we hire truly wants to give great service. Of every 100 people we bring in to work, roughly five are going to be great service providers whether they work at Zingerman's, the Ritz, the post office, or Northwest Airlines. That's just who they are. You've probably been waited on by one of them. You shop somewhere that consistently has horrific service and you come across one of these five friendly folks; amongst the gloom and doom, there they are, smiling and enthusiastically greeting guests and doing a great job no matter how glum their peers are. At the other end of the spectrum, another five of the 100 hires just aren't going to give good service no matter what. I don't care where they work or what they get paid, they just aren't going to do it. The effective leader is, of course, going to promote, recognize and reward the five great service givers, while removing the five subpar staffers ASAP.

Most of the time, though, I focus on the other 90 folks, because my experience is that they're going to go with the flow. Our job as leaders is to create an organizational structure that makes it much easier and much more rewarding for them to give great service than not. We make that flow happen by aligning all the elements of the Business Perspective Chart (see page 10) so that each actively encourages the giving of great service. In other words, when service is built into our mission,

where well-meaning service staff may slip

- They have difficulty backing down, especially when customers are wrong.

- They start trying to prove a point, one that may be correct, but in the process they end up leaving the customer fuming over the quality of the service interaction. We need to find ways to help customers feel happy and comfortable with a resolution, without making them feel like they were "wrong."

- They lose perspective—the customer starts to seem like an annoyance, or an obstacle to getting their "real work done." Ironically, this is particularly common when service staffers are dealing with long-term regular customers, the very same folks whose purchases probably pay a very high proportion of our wages.

- They don't see themselves as part of the organization and defer responsibility to others, rather than realizing that the quality of every interaction belongs to all of us, collectively.

when it's an essential element of our vision of success, when we measure it regularly, when we create service-oriented systems, when our values are focused on giving, and when our culture actively supports all of the above, then it's darned likely that those 90 folks in the middle are going to give great service. And in the end, they're the ones who are going to be waiting on a lot more of our customers than any single service star in our organization.

service vs. services

Although the quality of one's service and the services one offers are two very different things, the distinction often perplexes people who work in the service world. It's worth it to fight through the confusion:

If we can learn to distinguish between the two, we'll be much better-equipped to give great service to our customers and to reduce service-related stress on all involved. Here's my take:

"Service," as we use it at Zingerman's, refers to the quality of the interaction with one's clients. "Services," on the other hand, refers to what one provides to one's customers, such as catering, groceries, dinner, consulting, cleaning, or free delivery.

The challenge in this area usually comes when customers ask for "services" that we don't provide. What tends to happen in these situations is that the staffers are so dumbfounded by the off-the-wall thing the customer is asking for, they respond in a way that is at best unhelpful, or, at worst, downright rude.

What I've learned is that even the most seemingly outrageous request for services (note the "s" at the end there) that we don't provide can be handled with grace, allowing all involved to exit from a sensitive situation in a way that lets the customer keep their dignity and lets us keep a customer. Say, for instance, a customer calls Zingerman's and asks us to fly a private jet to Kentucky to pick up the customer's prized country ham. It would be an understandable reaction to say something along the lines of, "What, are you crazy? We don't fly private planes. We're in the food business!" Sadly, that's probably the way most service people in most companies would react. Even if they didn't use those words, it's not unlikely that their facial expressions or tone of voice would quickly give them away.

To me, the right response to this sort of inquiry is no different than handling a customer complaint in the manner I've outlined above. You simply follow those same five steps:

Acknowledge what the guest is saying: "Wow, you need a plane flown to Kentucky?!"

Then apologize: "I feel so bad. We aren't qualified to take on a responsibility like that—we just don't have any trained pilots on staff right now. But now that you've asked, it sounds like something we might consider down the road."

Then you try to make things right: "In the meantime, though, I'd be glad to go get the Yellow Pages and make a couple of phone calls. Let me see if we can't find a company around here that could help you. Would that be OK?" In this case, you're actually going the extra mile for the customer. (And if you're really good, you're going to learn more about the customer and what they do because anyone calling about corporate jets will also likely be a big corporate gift giver—and we want that business! And now that I think about it, I'd be sure to recommend some good food for their in-flight enjoyment as well.)

This scenario may sound crazy, but the truth is that it's not that far-fetched. Many service providers I know have had to handle stranger situations than this one. The point is, instead of telling the customer that they're crazy for asking for something so off-the-wall, simply apologize for not being able to fulfill their needs and then see if there's any way you can help them. In the end, you might make a long-term customer out of them. On the subject of opportunities to capitalize on, I will say that I've learned to pay close attention to seemingly strange situations like this one. Which, by the way, is all the more reason to document the complaints that come in ("Step 5" above) so that we can watch for relevant opportunities to cater to otherwise-unmet customer needs; also so that we can in the process, build ourselves a whole new way to increase sales, differentiate ourselves in the marketplace, and so on.

The easiest example of this that I can think of is overnight package and mail delivery. It's pretty much a given that consumers were interested in, and willing, to pay for a service of this sort for a long time, but that the primary service provider in the field—the post office— never saw fit to do anything about it. Then one day, Fred Smith had the idea of opening up FedEx. And, in no time at all, paying $10 or $12 to get an envelope from Evanston to East Jersey became a common occurrence.

what's a staff member to do when they think they're being harassed by a customer?

At Zingerman's, we serve thousands and thousands of people over the course of a year. In a few cases, we come in contact with guests who are almost abusive to our staff—people who go well beyond the point where

the staff member feels able to provide them with good service. When that happens, we find ourselves in a difficult position, but we still don't abandon our commitment to good service. Instead, we ask our staff to handle the situation as if it were a customer complaint:

A. Acknowledge that things are not going well for them.

B. Apologize for their frustration.

C. Rather than "making things right," tell the guest that they're going to have the manager come over right away to provide more effective assistance.

The manager will take it from there and hopefully find a graceful way out of the difficulty. If they can't, they'll repeat the above steps and turn things over to a partner. In most cases, just the involvement of an upper level manager—which people often perceive to be a sign of respect—will get the guest to calm down. However, in those few cases where it does not, and where we believe that a guest has demonstrated a consistent pattern of harassment, the partners will ultimately suggest that everyone involved would be better-served if we didn't do business together.

Note that even in this extreme situation, we would end the relationship in terms of not being willing to give poor service rather than blaming the guest for what we believe is inappropriate behavior. Why not set the guest "straight"? If things have gone on this long and the guest remains oblivious to the issues at hand, then they are clearly not ready to hear that their behavior is out of bounds. And again, we want to exit the situation as painlessly as possible. We don't want the customer out there in the community speaking ill of us—ironically and unfairly, it's typically the loud and obnoxious customer who is most likely to spread bad word-of-mouth most quickly. So I believe it's important not to act on the desire to give them a lecture on proper decorum, and instead simply get all those involved out of an uncomfortable position, as gracefully as possible.

Once every three or four years, we do come up against a situation where we make a decision that we aren't going to do business with a particular customer. Again, only partners are authorized to make that decision, and the situation must still be handled in a service-oriented way. Just as if we were firing a staff member (which should be done with dignity and respect), so too can we let a customer know that we'll no longer be serving them while communicating that message in a caring and courteous tone.

managing unrealistic customer expectations

Sometimes giving great service can be difficult because customers start out with expectations that exceed what we're able to deliver. This can be particularly true with big, emotionally-charged work.

For us, it's a challenge that comes up regularly with catering, consulting, and Christmas gift-giving, but I'm certain it's not unique to us. Let's say a customer comes in and wants an amazingly impressive sit-down dinner for 100 but has a budget of $500. Or they want us to come in and do a two-hour inspirational ZingTrain presentation on service for their front-line staff, when it's  pretty clear upper-level leadership itself hasn't bought in to the idea of service success. In these sorts of situations, we're headed for customer unhappiness.

Although it may be easy to deliver exactly what the customer has narrowly defined, the problem is that they probably aren't going to be happy about the results of the work after we've delivered it. With that in mind, although it may be more difficult in the moment, it's far more productive to engage the client in a lot of early dialogue to see if you can effectively adjust their expectations up front. Gentle, probing questions about desired outcomes can be helpful. So, too, is asking them if they've shopped around to check out any of the competition. Even though we're a high-end provider in our marketplace, we're not so far out of the ballpark that checking on the competition wouldn't help the guest to frame things for themselves.

If we can't help the client develop reasonable expectations, my belief is that we're probably better off not taking the business; it's almost certainly a set-up for failure and frustration on all sides. Now, don't misread that—I never walk away lightly from the chance to make a sale and line-up a good customer. I work really hard and happily use all of my creative skills and the skills of those around me to find a way that will work. But if I've tried to align our abilities with the client's expectations and I still feel like we're headed for trouble, I'm going to gently suggest that they're going to be disappointed in what we provide, and that I really don't want that to happen. Notice that I try to take the burden on us; basically, I sell them on why it will be better for them to work with someone else instead of dismissing them curtly or rudely. In fact, I might try to clinch things by going the extra mile and sending them a "thank you" note for even having considered us in the first place, and offering assistance again in the future. Even though they may not become a customer this time, they're still out there in the community, and the last thing I want is for them to speak badly of our organization.

improved service raises the bar

Another good problem that comes out of success is that if you sustain service improvement for any length of time, your customers' expectations are sure to rise. And, of course, the higher those expectations go, the harder it is to deliver a level of service that will really impress them time after time. I welcome this challenge, and try to be as up-front about it as I can within our organization. What we consider good service today will not be good enough two years from now. We know that we have to keep getting better at what we do. And we're very committed to doing so.

Opud vs. Upod

One thing I've learned to watch out for is the tendency of committed staff members to overpromise and underdeliver. This is never malicious. They simply want to "wow" their customers by giving the guest really quick turnaround or great pricing or something of that sort. The problem is that they're offering something that we can't deliver. Ironically, the problem is very often of our own making; in most of these cases, I've found that the customer wasn't even asking for the turnaround time the staff member was suggesting. Unfortunately, we're going to end up in big trouble because we've now got the guest waiting eagerly for something that we're going to fall short on. That's an OPUD—we've overpromised and are now underdelivering. What we want to do is the opposite—we want to UPOD. (Credit for this acronym goes to Bob Bohlen, who's done great service work in his real estate practice in Brighton, Michigan, and in the "Money Matters" seminars he puts on around the world.) That is, we want to underpromise and then overdeliver—in essence, going the extra mile by first setting reasonable expectations and then exceeding them!

being willing to break the rules

Have you ever had the experience that staff members will fail to follow the rules over and over again, except for the one time that you didn't want them to follow the rules because the rules were obviously wrong? It's a repetitive pattern that...well, to be blunt, makes me crazy! Policies adhered to for the sake of rule-following frequently punish innocent customers who weren't up to speed on our systems. So, while we certainly want our staff to adhere to our "rules," we also want them to think for themselves, to make decisions in the context of the Business Perspective Chart, and to understand and act on the reality that sometimes we have to break the rules or ignore the systems in the interest of taking care of our customers.

One way we work to combat this is to remind everyone who works here that our systems and rules are only set up to help to effectively get great service to our customers. And that when they need to, we want our staff to break the rules in order to give better service. With this in mind, we specifically address this in our Guiding Principles by saying that, "We understand that our actions have an impact on our customers. We retain the flexibility to make exceptions to our rules when it is in the best interests of our guests to do so. We do not hold our guests responsible for not being familiar with our systems."

What that means in practice is that we specifically ask our staff to be ready to break the rules in order to give better service to customers. We know that there are exceptions to every rule, and the last thing we want to do is handle our customers based on the law of averages. To the contrary, every customer wants special service. In fact, we specifically ask staffers here to find a way to "Just say yes!" to customers if there's any way we can possibly meet their needs (think out of the box here).

What does this look like in practice? We have one customer who comes into the Deli every Saturday. He's not the easiest guy in the world to deal with. He has very good taste and very high standards, and he's very particular about what he wants—or doesn't want—on any given day. Often, what he's in the mood for isn't on the menu. But instead of reading him the rules, we've adjusted the rules to fit his needs. Only a manager takes his order. A manager or a supervisor always prepares it. As a result, he's been coming back Saturday after Saturday for probably 15 years now. And because he's very vocal about his feelings, I know that he's out in the community telling people why they too should come and experience Zingerman's.

moments of truth!!

A "moment of truth" is the term that we use here to describe those situations where there's no overt customer complaint to be dealt with, but where, for whatever reason, we're about to lose a customer. We call it a "moment of truth" because given the right set of perceptive eyes to spot the problem and some effective turnaround work, we can save the situation, often making a customer for life out of someone who was pretty much halfway out the door.

What's a moment of truth look like? Well, the signs are probably different in every business. Here, it might be a customer walking in the front door of the Deli, looking around with a bit of a scowl because they don't see what they want, then turning and leaving without saying a thing. Often, we have what they're looking for, but our space is small and confusing, and much of what's available isn't very visible to the untrained customer. With that in mind, I've chased confused, first-time customers into the street to get them to come back inside.

Moments of truth are particularly important for leaders to be aware of, because the signals often run below the surface and are easily ignored by those who aren't experienced or who choose not to look for them. One customer saved through the successful identification and resolution of a moment of truth could mean the saving of thousands of dollars in sales over a period of years:

I've emailed potential Mail Order customers back and forth for weeks to find a way to get them to give us a chance, when at first it didn't seem as if we had what they wanted.

better Service can lead to more complaints

As I said before, strange as it may sound, if you do all of the above really well, you're actually going to encounter some "new" service issues—the kind of "problems" that poor-service providers rarely have to deal with. The truth is that the better the service your organiza-

tion gives, the more your customers and staff are going to hold you to high service standards. I know that here at Zingerman's, we hear customer complaints that almost no other business would encounter. People tell us about small lapses in service enthusiasm from new staff members, the slightest inconsistencies in a bread that they've bought over a period of months, or a single typo in a 10,000-word issue of our newsletter. As hard as it is for me to not get defensive when people raise these seemingly picky points, these sorts of complaints are really great praise for our organization. The vast majority of customers out there in the world won't waste the time or energy bothering to say anything: Most companies would kill to have customers who were that attuned to their products' finer points.

measuring it

setting up a scorecard for service

"Probably the single best word of mouth for a store is this: 'they're so nice down at that shop!' When service is poor, shoppers will find another store; bad service undoes good merchandise, prices and location almost every time."
—Paco Underhill, *Why We Buy; The Science of Shopping*

why measure?

Service measurement is an area of our work at Zingerman's that's changed significantly as our organization has grown and succeeded. When your company is small—a one-, two-, or ten-person team—there's really no huge need for measuring service quality. Successful owners of very small businesses have their fingers on the service pulse of whatever it is that they do. They're usually all too aware of where the mistakes have been made, and of who has—or has not—worked effectively to correct them. But as one's organization grows, it becomes increasingly important to gather data on service quality to supplement the good gut feeling that helped create success in the first place.

Only when we have some effective measurement can we really quantify how we're doing. Imagine you had no financial statements. You'd find yourself arguing with one of your managers over how the business was performing, but there'd be no data to back up either side! Without some measurement, an argument over service quality really becomes as unproductive as a disagreement over who knows best how to attain world peace. The discussion can go on forever, but you accomplish next to nothing in the process, other than wasting time.

Another important reason to track service experiences is to point out patterns and repetitive problems that might otherwise get missed. It's easy for me to imagine one committed service-giver encountering two very unhappy customers in any given week, both of whom complained about the quality of the service we gave over the phone. Without any additional data to go on, the staff member's perception is guaranteed to be that our phone service is really slipping. Is the staff member correct in her assumption? Well, she certainly has legitimate cause for concern, but whether she's right or not, I can't really say. If those were the only two complaints of that type to come in over a ten-week period, I'd say that we're probably doing fine on the phones, but that this one staff member happened to get stuck dealing with them both. Conversely, if 20 of us heard a single complaint on phone manners over the course of the same ten weeks, it would be extremely easy to dismiss what we'd heard as an isolated incident. But when we start to compile the data, it's glaringly clear that we've got a big problem on our hands.

One last point to make here: Without some standard of measurement that you can use to judge progress from year to year, it's very difficult to maintain one's sense of moving forward. For me at least, having some consistent measure gives me a tool that I can use to look back on our progress over time and get a much-needed sense of perspective. And in the emotional roller coaster that business can often be, that's a tool whose importance I don't underestimate.

service scores and forecasting for the future

I've often heard people say that you don't need to measure service quality. They argue that financial statements are all that really matter. "If you just watch the financials," they tell me, "you'll know if your service work is good." But from my experience, although service and finance are very much connected, success in one area does not directly follow the other. Good service doesn't guarantee great finance, nor does great finance today necessarily indicate that our levels of service have been great in the last few weeks. (One could more safely say that sales and service are correlated. Certainly, better service is likely to have a positive influence on sales. But while your service and sales may both be stellar, you could still be losing lots of money if you don't do good work on costing, pricing, and portioning.) Balance sheets, profit-and-loss and cash flow statements only tell you what's already happened. But when you read your service performance scores, they are very strong predictors of what is going to happen to your sales in the weeks and months to come. Quite clearly, customers who've had poor service are simply less likely to come back; when service scores start to fall off, I know that our sales are likely to follow a similar downward trend. Our experience here at Zingerman's has been consistent—drop-offs in service quality start to show up in the form of lower sales about six months after the service began to deteriorate. It's the same cycle for service improvement: The benefit of the good service work we do today will start to show up in sales increases five, six, or seven months from now.

how to measure service

The most important thing in tracking service quality is to pick a couple of measurements that work and simply start measuring. Don't wait forever while you try to determine the perfect ones, because truthfully, they don't exist. In fact, almost any solid measurement—taken consistently and reviewed regularly to spot trends and problems—is going to help.

I believe that, ideally, the most effective way to tackle service quality measurement is to track at least one item from each of the following three categories:

I. Directly measure customer response and satisfaction.

This is data that comes to us directly from clients.
It could include:

- Mystery shopping
- Customer surveys
- Call-backs to customers
- Customer roundtables
- On-time deliveries
- Customer complaints
- Order accuracy
- Customer compliments

If you only want to start with one area of measurement,
I'd make it something from this category, because it
keeps you closest to the customers.

**2. Monitor internal systems controls that lead
to better service.**

These are key performance measures that take place
before the actual product or service gets to the
customer, ones that we know are likely to lead to
better service. Such measures include:

- Consistently pre-checking our outgoing orders
- Deliveries leaving our location on time
  (as opposed to those that actually arrive at the
  client's location on time)
- Consulting proposals sent out on time
- Ensuring a short response time to customer
  complaints

While in and of themselves these sorts of measures don't guarantee good service, they can help us watch for possible problems before they cause serious service lapses at the customer's level. Quite clearly, if we're consistently late in leaving our site to make deliveries, it's darned likely that we will soon see an increase in late-delivery complaints as we collect data from customers through some of the means mentioned in number 1.

3. Recognize patterns that are indicators of past service success.

These usually indicate that customers are happy with what they're getting from us, and that we're doing a good job of serving them. Again, they don't in and of themselves measure actual service quality, but they're likely predictors of future successes or shortfalls. Some examples:

- Repeat orders
- Repeat customers
- Sales per customer, per year
- Average order size
- Customer referrals
- Customer compliments

As with the key types of financial statements—profit-and-loss, balance sheet, and cash flow—when considered alone, each one of these three methods of service measurement offers us only one dimension of a far more complex picture. Only when you measure in all three of these areas will you get a solid, holistic sense of how your group is performing.

what do you do with service measurements once you have 'em?

You do the same sorts of things that you'd do with financial measurements when they're used well:

- Review performance scores regularly so everyone knows how you're doing.
- Use them to drive your decision-making on systems implementation, promotions, hiring, and others.
- Tie bonus plans to service scores.
- Run group games with group rewards to help give your staff the incentive to improve service quality.
- Publish service ratings with the same regularity and seriousness that you would with your profit-and-loss statements.

I don't want to give the impression that measurement alone is going to solve all your service problems; nor would I ever advocate simply ignoring one's gut feelings in favor of gathering an excessive amount of data. It simply adds another valuable tool to your service-leadership toolbox, one that will allow you to temper and check your intuition against something a bit more objective.

rewarding it
appreciating great service givers

"Finally, the greatest job enrichment of all is your attitude. If you pay attention, listen, be accessible, open up and provide your people with as many special treatments and celebrations and learning experiences as you can, you'll be overwhelmed by the abundance of thinking all around you."
—Jim Autry, *Love and Profit*

recognizing and rewarding great service

Willingness to reward and recognize great service when it's given is essential. Hardly any of us gets too much positive reinforcement—and most everyone likes to get some acknowledgment and appreciation when they do good work.

The key in this regard is less what the perfect rewards are than it is that the organization makes an active effort in this area. My experience is that in many businesses, the top service providers get pretty much the same rewards that go to their peers who give poor service.

In fact, in many organizations the best service providers are "rewarded" with more work—they're so good at waiting on customers that everyone else gets out of the way and lets them wait on more people than ever!

If you already have a program for doing this, keep going! If you don't have one yet, start soon. Effectively rewarding great service will work best when you use a combination of both informal recognition and more clearly defined games and bonus plans that are tied to service. There's no perfect formula. Some of the things we do at Zingerman's include:

- Publishing "X-tra Mile Files" each month in Workin', our staff newsletter, in order to give recognition to those in the organization who are going out of their way to do those little extra things to make our service exceptional. Winners get a special X-tra Mile T-shirt.
- Giving a "Green Machine" award each month to the staff member who writes up the most Code Greens.
- Giving out monthly "Service Star Awards" to those who give great service day-in and day-out. Both the service provider and the person who nominated the winner get financial rewards.
- Publishing a couple of pages of "Thank Yous and Bravos" each month in the staff newsletter to help keep the appreciative spirit alive within the organization.

- Running group games around our mystery shopping scores.
- Tying bonuses to service measurements.

Don't underestimate the value of something as simple as a handwritten "thank you" note from you as a leader to a great service provider. Little things like that make a huge difference in building the sort of culture of positive appreciation, attention to detail and caring that we're working to create.

SERVICE STARS!

Christine Krause (a.k.a. "Turkey Chaos Coordinator")
Nominated by Todd Wickstrom

Chris was very instrumental to all of the success we had with our Heritage Turkey program. When others bailed on the project and any responsibility associated with it, not because of a lack of commitment but as a result of just being crazy-busy like the rest of us, Chris picked up the ball and not only ran with it, but scored multiple touchdowns. She went way and above the call of duty making and taking long distance calls from all over the country, confirming all of the orders, being sure they were all accounted for financially and even helping to distribute them from our Pre-Paid Pick-Up tent on the day before Thanksgiving. All of this was done above and beyond her everyday responsibilities of keeping the Deli office running smoothly. She didn't just help make my life easier during this time, she helped our local Slow Food convivium, Slow Food USA, the Heritage Turkey Farmers, the future of the whole program and maybe most importantly, helped to ensure that literally hundreds of people across the country enjoyed the tastiest turkey of their lives! Thanks for giving such great service to not only the ZCoB, Christine, but a whole bunch of food-lovin' folks across the country!

final thoughts

it's still one customer at a time

"Given the chance, people will buy from people who care."
—Paco Underhill,
Why We Buy: The Science of Shopping

Having gone on at length about the various theoretical and practical elements of giving great service, about the value of clarity and a coherent structure, training, and active measurement, I want to wrap up by reminding myself and everyone else that great service is still given—and will always be given—one customer at a time. Though statistics and systems are great, it's imperative to remember that unless you have an ad budget the size of the state of Texas, you aren't going to win over customers in demographic segments. They come in, are engaged, and are won over one by one. Seemingly small things like going the extra mile, remembering customers' names, noticing a nice order and saying "thanks," taking time to show a new customer around our place of business—those individual acts are still the things that make great service a reality.

Just recently I met a couple at the Deli who told me that although they'd lived in the Ann Arbor area for 40 years, they'd never been to Zingerman's until that morning. They'd heard of us but had never driven the 20 minutes to visit in person.

As always, I was in the middle of about 15 things and sort of in a hurry to get back to work. But having taught the "one customer at a time" approach so often, I couldn't just walk away in good conscience. So I did what we teach everyone to do: I engaged the customer and spent more time talking to them.

As we talked, I noticed that all they'd ordered were a couple cups of coffee and a single muffin. While I'm sure the coffee and the muffin were very good, I wasn't convinced that those items alone were going to create the kind of memorable first experience that can win over customers for life. So I offered to get them a packet of Zingerman's literature. They accepted the offer, and I brought over our Deli menu, ZingTrain brochure, Catering Guide, newsletter, and Mail Order catalog.

For the next 20 minutes, they sat, drinking coffee and reading through each of the brochures, commenting to each other about one item or another in the copy. Since they were obviously interested in what we do, I thought that this would be a great time to really solidify our new relationship. So I grabbed one of our little Sourcream Coffeecakes—a product everyone loves, hence a safe item to send a newcomer home with—and said that I wanted to give it to them to help welcome them to Zingerman's. They graciously told me that I didn't have to do that. I, of course, acknowledged that I didn't have to, but kindly insisted. We kept talking, and they proceeded to tell me that they really loved the Mail Order catalog. The husband was also very intrigued by ZingTrain; he works for a good-sized computer firm and was interested in service training and some of the other items we offer.

Finally, they got up to go, and told me they were headed over to the main building of the Deli to buy some bread. Again, I thanked them for coming down. "We'll be back!" they said, smiling. And I'm sure they will.

I tell this story not because I want you to think I did a great job, but because this is the best way I know of to take service and turn it into a positive tool for making a difference. The couple left with a much better introduction to Zingerman's than they probably expected as a result of the time we spent together. I'm confident that their morning was a bit more interesting and enjoyable, and I can almost guarantee that in one form or another—more than likely—they're going to come back.

The bottom line here is that the work each of us does as an individual service provider with an individual customer—one interaction at a time—is what it's all about. From both a personal and a business perspective, I truly appreciate the opportunity to make such a difference a reality.

Ari

appendix handy service tools

zingerman's guiding principles

1) great food

At Zingerman's, we are committed to making and selling high-quality food. Great food at Zingerman's means:

We are a food-driven business.

While we engage in many activities at Zingerman's, first and foremost we are in business to sell food.

Flavor in our food comes first.

We choose our products first and foremost on the basis of flavor. We sell food that tastes great.

Our foods have tradition.

We sell foods that have roots, a heritage, a history. We seek out traditionally-made, frequently hand-crafted foods which are primarily of peasant origin.

We work to sell our food at the peak of its flavor

Traditionally made foods are alive and different everyday. They are affected by weather, soil, climate, the skill and craft of the producer, and the care and handling by our staff. We regularly taste and evaluate our products in order to assure our guests of the most flavorful food possible.

Good food makes life more fun.

We value the pleasure one gets from savoring a sliver of fine farmhouse cheddar, or from the aroma of an aged balsamic vinegar. We value the opportunity to sell and enjoy so many fine foods.

Good food is for everyone, not just a select few.

We make our food accessible to as many people as possible. We put our guests at ease with our food. No advanced degrees are needed to appreciate it—just a willingness to taste and experience the pleasure it provides. To that end, we will gladly offer a taste of our foods to our guests.

Our foods look great.

Our food always looks neat, fresh, appealing, eye-catching. A just-split wheel of Parmigiano-Reggiano, a just-off-the-grill Georgia Reuben (#18) are sights to behold. We work to present them to our guests simply and effectively. We display our food in abundance to demonstrate both our commitment to the food, and to convey that at Zingerman's, our food comes first.

2) great service

If great food is the lock, great service is the key. Great service at Zingerman's means:

We go the x-tra mile, giving exceptional service to each guest.

We are committed to giving great service—meeting the guests' expectations and then exceeding them. Great service like this is at the core of the Zingerman's Experience.

Our bottom line is derived from customer satisfaction.

Customer satisfaction is the fuel that stokes the Zingerman's fire. If our guests aren't happy, we're not happy. The customer is never an interruption in our day.

We welcome feedback of all sorts. We constantly reevaluate our performance to better accommodate our customers. Our goal is to have our guests leave happy. Each of us takes full responsibility for making our guest's experience an enjoyable one before, during and after the sale.

We believe that giving great service is an honorable profession.

Quality service is a dignified and honorable pursuit. We take great pride in our ability to provide our guests and our staff with exceptional service. Service is about giving and caring for those around us.

We give great service to each other, as well as to our guests.

We provide the same level of service to our peers as we do our guests. We are polite, supportive, considerate, superb listeners, and always willing to go the x-tra mile for each other.

3) a great place to shop and eat!
Coming to Zingerman's is a positive and enjoyable experience for our guests.

We surround our guests with great food, great energy and great experiences.

The guest's first exposure to Zingerman's is a breathtaking experience: food, energy and excitement are everywhere. The aromas of fine food waft through the air.

We provide a dazzling environment for our customers and staff.

It's neat! It's clean! It's Zingerman's! Floors are swept and mopped constantly, windows sparkle, employees fall to the floor, colliding with each other as they race to clear each table before the guest has hardly moved away from it.

We follow safe food-handling procedures.

Handling food carries with it responsibility for the health and well-being of our guests. We are well-informed on safe food-handling procedures and implement them consistently in every area of our work.

Our policies and systems help the businesses run better.

We understand that our actions have an impact on our customers. With this in mind, we retain the flexibility to make exceptions to our rules when it is in the best interest of our guests to do so. We do not hold our guests responsible for not being familiar with our systems.

4) Solid Profits

Profits are the lifeblood of our business.

We operate at a healthy level of profit.

Profits provide us with security and growth potential in order to fulfill our mission. Attaining healthy profits requires a concerted and consistent contribution from everyone at Zingerman's. Toward that end, we educate our entire staff about the financial workings of the business.

We want to make our profit work for our staff, our growth, and our community, as well as for the businesses.

We reinvest our profits in the business. We share profits

with the staff. We give back to our community through donations of money, time and products.

We are committed to being fiscally responsible in our work.

We spend according to our means. We are willing to delay gratification in order to build long-term rewards.

We are a growth business.

We are committed to healthy, productive expansion and growth of our sales, consistent with our mission and our principles.

5) a great place to work

Working at Zingerman's means taking an active part in running the business. Our work makes a difference.

We are empowered by the creativity, hard work and commitment of our staff.

It is the energy, effort and involvement of our staff that help make Zingerman's successful.

We are committed to each other's success.

Each of us is committed to the success of everyone else who works at Zingerman's.

We compensate our staff well.

We provide income, a benefits package, profit sharing, meaningful work, and a sense of community for our staff.

We provide opportunity for growth and advancement.

We actively work to provide for the healthy growth of our business. In so doing, we provide opportunities for staff who wish to grow within Zingerman's.

We involve as many people as possible in the running of the business.

We bring as many people as practical into the operation of the business. In so doing, Zingerman's runs more effectively, benefiting from everyone's abilities, creativity, experience and intelligence.

Each of us is committed to being proactive in our work.

We aggressively tackle difficult issues without waiting to be asked. We know that each of us bears the responsibility for what goes on around us.

We work to improve in every area.

We seek to improve our performance, individually and as a group, and work to our fullest potential, through self-reflection, education, cooperation and feedback from others. When something is not working, we look at ourselves to improve before we look at the work of others. We do so as individuals, as departments and businesses.

We learn from our errors and work to correct them.

When we make mistakes, we view them as opportunities for growth and change. When we make an error we do not seek to assign blame, rather, we try to avoid repeating the problem in the future.

We strive to create a safe workplace.

We work within the limits of our historic space to create a safe workplace. We continually reevaluate and act to improve our work space. We walk slowly and carefully on the stairs, we never leave knives unattended in the sink, we pay close attention at all times when using slicers. We catch each other when we fall.

Zingerman's embraces diversity.

We go out of our way to build a diverse and well-balanced workplace. We hire individuals regardless of race, religion, gender or sexual preference.

We like to have fun.

And we take our fun very seriously. So don't mess with it.

6) Strong realationships!

Successful working relationships are an essential component of our health and success as a business.

We build long-term relationships with our customers.

The long-term relationships with our guests are more important to us than any short-term transaction or interaction. To that end, we go the x-tra mile to take care of our guests and their families; we learn their tastes, their favorite sandwiches, their shopping needs.

We are committed to long-term working relationships with our staff.

We build mutually rewarding and long-term relationships with our staff. We work to retain those positive relationships even after one of our staff has chosen to leave Zingerman's.

We establish rewarding relationships with our suppliers.

We view our relationships with our suppliers as a partnership in which both sides benefit. Our dealings are based on courtesy and consideration.

We build connections with other businesses who share similar values.

We seek out like-minded businesses to develop an effective support network for ourselves. We work with them to share information and ideas.

We celebrate group achievement and recognize individual success.

We regularly go out of our way to enjoy and recognize our accomplishments as a business. When one of us is successful we are all successful.

7) a place to learn!

Learning keeps us going, keeps us challenged, keeps us on track.

We educate our guests, staff and ourselves about the food we sell.

We believe that the more we learn about food (where it comes from, how it's made, how to use it), the more effectively and profitably the business will operate.

We actively educate our staff about the workings of the business.

We regularly share business information with our staff. The more we understand about the business the more productive we will be.

We actively educate ourselves about all aspects of our jobs.

We consistently seek to improve our understanding

of our own jobs by staying current in industry literature, and attending conferences and trade shows.

8) an active part of our community

We believe that a business has an obligation to give back to the community of which it is a part.

We participate in improving life in our community.

We actively work to make our community a better place to live by contributing time, food, money, energy and information.

We encourage our staff to participate in community service.

We encourage our staff members to contribute to their community, to be active citizens, to work to better their environment.

We're here to stay.

We're committed to building long-lasting, mutually beneficial relationships with our city, our neighborhood, and our community. We are committed to a long-term business strategy that will keep us in our community for many years to come.

6 steps to effective telephone service at zingerman's

Since we do so much of our business over the phone, it's imperative that we give the best, most-professional service possible whenever we are on the phone, just as we would to a guest standing right in front of us. So...

1. If the phone is ringing, answer it.
This may seem obvious, but if you don't answer the phone, you lose business. Not answering the phone is like ignoring a guest standing at the counter waiting to order.

2. Body language speaks volumes.
The person on the other end of the line may not be able to see us, but nevertheless our body language and attitude are clearly conveyed over the phone. Smiling and sitting upright can make a very positive difference in the quality of one's phone service. You really can "hear" the smile over the phone—this is so true it's scary!

3. Politeness counts.
When we're working on the phone, courtesy counts even more than it does in person. Be careful to convey patience and gratitude for the guests' business at all times. Our technique is a simple, sincere, and enthusiastic: "Good morning, thank you for calling Zingerman's. How may I help you?" Don't underestimate the importance of politeness and enthusiasm on the phone.

4. "May I please put you on hold?" is a question, not a statement.
Be sure to give the guest a chance to answer this question before you put them on hold.

5. Accuracy and attention to detail are critical.
As per our "4 Steps to Order Accuracy," we ask staff members to always read back an order to the guest in order to avoid mistakes. If guests phone-in an order for pick-up, we can go the extra mile by telling them where and when they can pick it up, or by inquiring if they need directions to our site.

6. End every call by thanking the guest.
After all, there are plenty of other providers they could have contacted instead of us and we appreciate the opportunity to serve them.

mirrors in marquette

One of the funniest phone-service stories I've ever heard came when I presented on the subject of service to northern Michigan's Upper Peninsula Council on Tourism. At the end of my talk, the gentleman who was the head of the Tourist Board for the town of Marquette came over to tell me how much he enjoyed the material, and to share a personal story about phone-service success. Mind you, if you don't know Michigan geography, Marquette is about as far from anything as you're going to get. Needless to say, they don't get a whole lot of walk-in traffic at the Marquette Tourist Office. In fact, nearly all of the work they do is over the phone.

The fellow told me that in order to help remind his staff to smile when they were on the phone, he'd placed small mirrors on each of their desks: The technique worked well, raising the level of their already-good service even higher. But one day when he was showing an out-of-towner around the office, at the end of his little tour his guest smiled and said, "Well, you've certainly got a great thing going. But," he added quizzically, "you sure have a lot of vain people working here!"

giving exceptional service to the disabLed, the eLderLy, or those in need of special attention

Though it may seem challenging, giving service to the disabled, elderly, or people with small children is not that different from giving service to any of our other guests. We still need to identify their needs, we still need to get them what they've asked for, and we still need to exceed their expectations and go the extra mile. When waiting on guests with special needs, we are more than happy to alter our systems and routines to accommodate them—if they'd prefer. It's important that we ask the guest if they want us to do so, however. Many people with disabilities take great pride in being able to work their way successfully through the world without any special treatment. And those folks are inevitably, understandably, offended by any action that singles them out. Our job, as per "Step 1" in our "3 Steps to Great Service," is to ask the guest how we can best serve them.

From a leadership perspective, our goal is to prepare staff for the likely possibility that, sooner or later, they will be serving people with special needs. When that moment comes, they will have some sense of how to deal with the situation in an appropriate, service-oriented manner.

With that in mind, here are a few of the ways we are able to serve guests with special needs at Zingerman's:

- Offer to review menu selections verbally to help someone who cannot read.
- Offer a braille menu for our Deli customers.
- Offer foreign language menu for our Deli customers.
- Offer to cut food into small pieces for someone who has physical disabilities.
- Open doors for anyone who has difficulty doing so.
- Offer to find someone who speaks the guest's language.

some simple stuff we don't do at zingerman's

NEVER respond to a guest's request with, "It's over there." Rather, take them to the area they are looking for.

NEVER respond to a guest's request with, "It's not my job." Instead, find someone who can effectively help them.

NEVER respond to a guest's request with, "I can't do that for you." Instead, find someone or something that will meet their needs. One way or another, we're going to help them out!

NEVER let a guest wait without acknowledging him or her. Just smile and say, "We'll be right with you," while you finish what you're doing for another guest.

NEVER say, "Anything else?" or "Is that all?" Instead ask, "What else can I get for you?"

10 tips for giving great service to guests who are hard of hearing or deaf

All of the tips or techniques below fit within our existing "3 Steps to Great Service." In that context, these tips merely provide us with ways to better implement those "3 Steps" when working with hard-of-hearing or deaf guests.

1. Every customer gets special attention.

Remember that every guest who is hard-of-hearing or deaf is an individual who will want the same sort of personalized service as all other guests. Be aware that some guests with hearing loss will give cues that they are uncomfortable with that loss being acknowledged. Back off when you sense this after any direct reference to a hearing loss.

2. Get the customer's visual attention.

We recommend starting the dialogue with a statement that's not essential to the issue. Politely ascertain that you've gotten the guest's attention by making some sort of eye contact before you start to talk. If they're looking somewhere else, it may be wise to pause until they turn back and reestablish visual contact. It's important to keep up that visual contact throughout the dialogue—this lets them know that you're talking to them, it helps them to focus on what you're saying, and it allows those who speech-read to do so more easily.

3. Keep your face toward the guest.
In order to ease the burden on the guest, it's important not to cover your mouth while talking; doing so makes it difficult for anyone who is hard-of-hearing or deaf to keep up with what you're saying, and also very difficult for them to speech-read. Similarly, please don't turn your back to the guest or speak to the floor. It's best to keep your lips in full view throughout the interaction.

4. Keep a steady tone of voice.
Sometimes the modulations of voice that we would normally use with customers who aren't hard-of-hearing make things more difficult for those who are. Be conscious of not lowering your voice. At the same time, don't shout—this can be embarrassing for the guest, and potentially as difficult for them to understand as if you were mumbling. If you're in doubt about appropriate volume levels for speaking, simply ask.

Similarly, it's important to speak at a regular or slightly slower pace than usual. Still, don't slow down too much—

if we vary our speech patterns too far from the normal flow of conversation, we can make it even more difficult for the guest to decipher what you're saying.

5. Avoid backlighting.
When you position yourself to the guest, be careful not to stand so that the customer has to face a bright light from behind you. This places a shadow on your face and makes it difficult to read lips and facial expressions.

6. Avoid saying, "never mind."
You may find that your customer was unable to understand something fairly unimportant that you've said to them. Try to avoid saying "never mind." In an instance where you've repeated yourself and the guest still does not hear what you've said, consider phrasing things in a different way.

7. Find a quiet spot.
If you're in a loud or hectic location, it may be appropriate to ask the guest if it would be easier to go to a quieter location to take their order. Be sensitive—some customers will appreciate the opportunity, while others will take great pride in not needing to do so.

8. Better body language may help.
Pointing to products, their signage, and names on printed materials, as well as using stronger facial expressions and shifting

your body when changing subjects, are examples of ways we can help customers with hearing loss. Be mindful, though, of not going overboard with exaggerated behavior that might bring unwanted attention or come across as patronizing.

9. Check frequently for understanding.

You can do this by repeating back parts of your conversation and asking politely for the customer to confirm that they've understood you and that you're both in agreement on next steps. In some instances, the guest you're working with may defer to a companion, and confer with him or her using either ASL (American Sign Language) or a foreign language. In this case, it's important not to cut the original customer out of the conversation, but rather to continue to speak directly to the guest with the hearing loss or language difficulty.

10. Writing may work best.

For some people—both deaf and hard-of-hearing—written communication will be the easiest manner of communica-tion. Simply and politely offer to write on a pad so that they can read your questions on paper. This can be done by asking the guest, "Would it be easier for you if I jotted some of these names down on paper?"

10 easy action steps to take to improve service in your organization

1. Review your recipe for great service and what it means in practical terms. Give concrete examples so that staffers are clear on what you're looking for.

2. Role play—it works. It's goofy. It's fun. It gets the point across. Certify people for service positions, or qualify them through bonuses, with role playing. A guy I used to work with would always ask, "How can we be a great team if we never practice?" He had a good point. When does your team practice giving service? (If you've got a slow moment, practice service scenarios instead of discussing "How we screwed up.")

3. Tell service stories. The knowledge of things that staffers do to provide guests with great service needs to be shared. People like to hear stories. When someone does something great in the course of giving service, don't keep it a secret.

4. Model it. Remember, if you're in a leadership role of any sort, everyone looks at the way you handle difficult situations. You set the tone.

5. Ask your staffers if they know your recipe for service success. Just asking shows that you put a priority on service.

6. If you're in a leadership role in your organization, remember that part of the job is to serve the staff as well as the guests.

7. Address the issue of fairness. This seems to be a big hang-up for many folks when they deal with service. Acknowledging that it's an issue will help staff members give up their attachment to "fairness" more effectively.

8. Include your recipe for service success in interviewing, early training tests, orientation classes, and so on, so that new staff members are getting a clear and consistent message on the subject of service, right off the bat.

9. Award and reward the great service people you work with.

10. Find a customer and do something special for them. Send them home with a smile and a fond memory of your service work.

5 simple hiring tips for service-oriented organizations

1) If an applicant doesn't smile during the interview, don't hire them.

2) Be sure that every job description and posting you put out mentions customer service.

3) Ask the applicant to describe some difficult service situations they've encountered, and to explain how they made the customer happy.

4) Role-play a customer complaint during the interview.

5) Ask service-oriented questions on your job application.

what is zingerman's anyway?

In 1982, Ari Weinzweig and Paul Saginaw opened
Zingerman's Delicatessen in Ann Arbor, Michigan. Their
intention was to offer a world-class corned beef sandwich in a retail space where guests would be surrounded
by exceptional food. Thirty years later, and still rooted in
Ann Arbor, Zingerman's Community of Businesses (ZCoB)
employs over 580 people and generates annual sales of
$50 million.

Zingerman's DELICATESSEN

From its inception, Zingerman's Delicatessen has been
committed to delivering the most flavorful, traditionally-made foods to its customers, presented in an enter-
taining, educational and service-oriented setting. We
have always believed that our customers can tell the
difference between mediocre and marvelous. The fact
that while competition increases every day, great
numbers of food-loving folks continue to find their way
down to Detroit Street to eat just reinforces that belief.
734.663.DELI (3354)

In 1992, Zingerman's Bakehouse opened, bringing traditionally-baked breads and pastries to Ann Arbor and Zingerman's customers across the country. The Bakehouse has an on-site Bakeshop which sells baked goods to retail customers, and has opened a teaching bakery called BAKE! 734.761.2095

Zingerman's Training Inc., a.k.a. ZingTrain, shares Zingerman's expertise in training, service, merchandising, specialty foods, and staff management with the public through seminars and one-on-one consulting. 734.930.1919

Zingerman's mail order

Zingerman's Mail Order sends extraordinary, traditionally-made foods across the country and around the world. Ed Behr, writing in *The International Wine Cellar*, referred to the company as "...the most discriminating mail order selection of foods that I am aware of." 888.636.8162

Zingerman's Creamery is dedicated to bringing fabulous-tasting, hand-crafted fresh cheeses, boldly-flavorful Italian-style gelato and much more to dairy lovers everywhere. 734.929.0500

Zingerman's Roadhouse is a casual, full-service restaurant that brings food-loving folks really good American food. 734.663.FOOD (3663)

Zingerman's Coffee Company roasts estate-grown and single origin coffees available in stores and cafés around the country as well as in our coffee bar in Ann Arbor. 734.929.6060

Zingerman's Candy Manufactory makes the Zzang!® candy bars called "the ultimate hand-made candy bar" by *Chocolatier Magazine.* 734.277.1922

Zingerman's Cornman Farms is a working farm, educational destination, and event venue. 734.619.8100

Zingerman's Catering puts together the simply sensational for both small parties and large events—serving everything from corned beef to caviar, charcuterie to champagne, party platters to Bakehouse wedding cakes. 734.663.3400

ari's biography

Ari Weinzweig
Founding Partner, Zingerman's

Ari Weinzweig is CEO and co-founding partner of Zingerman's Community of Businesses, which includes Zingerman's Delicatessen, Bakehouse, Creamery, Catering, Mail Order, ZingTrain, Coffee Company, Roadhouse, Candy Manufactory and the newest business— Cornman Farms. Zingerman's produces and sells all sorts of full flavored, traditional foods in its home of Ann Arbor, Michigan to the tune of $50,000,000 a year in annual sales. Ari was recognized as one of the "Who's Who of Food & Beverage in America" by the 2006 James Beard Foundation and has awarded a *Bon Appetit* Lifetime Achievement Award among many recognitions. Ari is the author of a number of articles and books, including *Zingerman's Guide to Better Bacon, Zingerman's Guide to Giving Great Service, Zingerman's Guide to Good Eating, Zingerman's Guide to Good Leading, Part 1: A Lapsed Anarchist's Approach to Building a Great Business,* and *Zingerman's Guide to Good Leading, Part 2: A Lapsed Anarchist's Approach to Being a Better Leader.* His most recent book, *Zingerman's Guide to Good Leading, Part 3: A Lapsed Anarchist's Approach to Managing Ourselves,* was released in December of 2013.

thanks and appreciations

The reality of giving service is that thousands of great customers and staff have patiently allowed us to "practice" on them over the last twenty-odd years. Without their support, assistance, constructive feedback and willingness to give us second and third opportunities to make things right when we've erred, the Zingerman's Community of Businesses wouldn't exist today. With that in mind, thanks so much to everyone who's participated in helping to make our service and service training what it is.

Thanks as always to the writing group: Deborah Bayer, Mabelle Hsui, Mort Cohn, and Lisa Walker for all their support and editing work over the years. Thanks to Laurel for everything. Thanks to Nicole, Ian, Holly, Phil and Adam for their design and marketing skills, and for being so much fun to work with. Thanks to all the partners at Zingerman's: Paul Saginaw, Frank Carollo, Maggie Bayless, Amy Emberling, Mo Frechette, Tom Root, John Loomis, Toni Morell, Rodger Bowser, Rick Strutz, Charlie Frank, Grace Singleton, Aubrey Thomason, Steve Mangigian, Kieron Hales, and Alex Young. Particular appreciation to Maggie, Stas', and ZingTrain for all the years of work that have gone into creating the training tools that have made it possible to put this service stuff into such a teachable, and I hope learnable, format. Thanks to everyone at Zingerman's who teaches service, including all of the above-mentioned partners, and special recognition to Kathi Dvorin, one of our all-time great service providers who regularly inspires me to ever-greater service heights. And thanks to Jenny Tubbs for leading the way to better customer service measurement through the now well-established-in-our-culture Code Red and Green Project.

Finally, thanks to everyone at Zingerman's for all your support, encouragement and enthusiasm, and for giving me the opportunity to work in such a special organization.